THE JUBILEE

The Jubilee

Enoch J Lavender

Contents

Foreword	xiii
Introduction	xv
Updated and Revised Edition	xvii
Jesus and the Jubilee	1
1 The Jubilee Concept	3
2 The Jubilee Messiah	11
3 The Miracles of the Jubilee	17
4 The Hope of Redemption	25
The End Times and the Jubilee	31
5 The Trumpet of Mt. Sinai	33
6 Introducing The Resurrection	37
7 Martha's Hope	45
8 The Final Victory	55
9 The Upside-Down Kingdom	61
10 Regathering The Exiles	73
11 The Gathering of the Saints	87
12 The Restoration Has Begun	97
13 The Divine Calendar	109
14 The God Who Doesn't Give Up	121
15 Back to the Garden	127

Appendixes — 139

16 Appendix A: Calculating the End — 141

17 Appendix B: The Second Resurrection — 145

18 Appendix C: The Parallel Restoration — 149

Index of Topics — 155
Selected Bibliography — 159
Other Books by the Author — 161
About the Author — 165

The Jubilee: Discover The End Time Mystery by Enoch Lavender, is a book that sheds light on God's kindness, promises and hope of redemption as we approach the very end of days. It reveals the heart of God, the patience of God, the prophecies of God, the compassion of God and His heart for His people. This book opened new doors of understanding for me and I pray it does the same for you.

Bishop Joseph Hopewell,
Apostolic Bishop
Co-founder of the Greater Life Church, Edinburgh, Scotland.
Co-founder and overseer of the Becoming Greater Television Channels

The church, the ekklesia, not only needs a new wineskin, it needs a new mind-skin. Enoch's book is a welcome and necessary challenge to the established mindset about the end-times! This book will help readers discover language and destiny that are more victorious than scary—to give a future and a hope!

A re-read of the book of Revelation you will discover the jubilant Biblical attitude as encouraged by Enoch's book. The dragon is defeated in both heaven and on earth! We must learn to speak the language of heaven rather than the language of fear driven apocalyptic annihilation.

Ruth Webb
Director and Prophetic Psalmist
Tabernacle of David House of Prayer Bendigo

The Jubilee takes you on an in-depth yet wonderfully clear explanation of an event that represents the core of the gospel: setting the captives free. Replete with sound interpretation and rounded off with practical application, Enoch Lavender is proclaiming a message that deserves to be heard.
Dr Kameel Majdali
Director
Teach All Nations

The Jubilee: Discover the End Time Mystery, Revised Edition
Copyright © 2024 by Enoch Lavender
ISBN 978-0-6450930-8-7
EISBN 978-0-6450930-9-4

Originally published as *The Jubilee: Discover the End Time Mystery* in 2023 by Olive Tree Ministries.

All rights reserved. No parts of this book may be reproduced in any form or by any means, electronic, mechanical, photocopying, scanning, or otherwise, without permission in writing from the publisher, except brief quote passages in a review.

Unless otherwise stated, biblical quotations are from the New King James Version. Copyright © 1982 by Thomas Nelson, Inc. Used by permission. All rights reserved.

Scripture quotations marked (NIV) are taken from the Holy Bible, New International Version®, NIV®. Copyright © 1973, 1978, 1984, 2011 by Biblica, Inc.TM Used by permission of Zondervan. All rights reserved worldwide. www.zondervan.com The "NIV" and "New International Version" are trademarks registered in the United States Patent and Trademark Office by Biblica, Inc.TM

Scripture taken from the Common English Bible®, CEB® Copyright © 2010, 2011 by Common English Bible.TM Used by permission. All rights reserved worldwide. The "CEB" and "Common English Bible" trademarks are registered in the United States Patent and

Trademark Office by Common English Bible. Use of either trademark requires the permission of Common English Bible.

Scripture taken from THE MESSAGE. Copyright © 1993, 1994, 1995, 1996, 2000, 2001, 2002. Used by permission of NavPress Publishing Group

Scripture taken from the Complete Jewish Bible by David H. Stern. Copyright © 1998. All rights reserved. Used by permission of Messianic Jewish Publishers, 6120 Day Long Lane, Clarksville, MD 21029. www.messianicjewish.net.

Scripture quotations marked (GNT) are from the Good News Translation in Today's English Version- Second Edition Copyright © 1992 by American Bible Society. Used by Permission.

To my Lord who has personally shown me His heart of restoration.
To my lovely wife Sarah who has supported me during many late nights of writing this book.
And with special thanks to First Fruits of Zion and Ps. Greg Cumming for their insightful teachings which have inspired this book.

Foreword

'When do you think Jesus is coming back?' As a pastor, I've been asked that question many times. I have often wondered what people are really wanting to discover when they ask that question? Are they after a specific date to put in their calendar? Are they checking on my theology to see if I am 'right'? Probably. Are they seeking confirmation of their own end time views?

The doctrine of end time events, commonly called 'eschatology', is a complex and often confusing area of study. Today, nearly two thousand years after the Apostle Paul penned: *'For the Lord Himself will descend from heaven with a shout'* (1 Thes. 4:16), more than a thousand writers have presented their views on the subject of end times to the world. And those views have been re-presented by itinerant preachers in all nations, and consequently converted into movies, tv shows and a plethora of YouTube videos.

But only a handful of people have really explored the underlying theology - and by underlying theology I don't mean a few short quotes from the New Testament.

When the foundational principles of the Torah and the prophets are combined with the words of Jesus and the apostles - and then considered in light of established Jewish messianic expectations - a picture begins to emerge that is slightly different to what we have been previously fed. This emerging picture of the end times is what I personally consider a more foundational, robust and reliable eschatology.

Ps. Enoch Lavender has succeeded in making these big foundational links in his work *The Jubilee: Discover the End Time Mystery*.

In the pages that follow, you will embark on an intelligent historical and spiritual journey exploring the timeless wisdom of the concept of the Biblical Jubilee. As Ps. Enoch unfolds the many layers of truth on this subject, we will begin to discover together just how central this ancient principle is - and how intricately it is woven into the teachings of Jesus, shaping what he calls *The Upside Down Kingdom*.

We will begin to see how the Jubilee relates to the Divine calendar, which in-turn informs major Biblical concepts such as the Coming of Messiah and the Regathering of Israel.

We discover that we too can adopt a Jubilee mindset and begin to interpret correctly Biblical truths and current events with a view to the ultimate restoration and renewal to come.

As you launch forward into this much needed book, and engage with each chapter, my prayer is that you may uncover the timeless relevance of the Jubilee and its enduring impact on our lives.

Ps. Greg Cumming
Good News For Israel

Introduction

I still remember the day when our youth group screened a movie on the End Times. The full length feature film spent most of its 90 minutes following the rise of a truly evil antichrist, with the good guy in the movie being powerless to stop him. Finally at the very end of the movie, a blinding white light appeared and the antichrist was finally defeated by the coming of Jesus. The movie left all of us in our small youth group pretty scared and shellshocked, with one girl in particular being close to tears.

Many Christians carry a dark foreboding sense of the End Times. They feel like evil will inevitably take over and run this world and there is little use to try to stop its progress. They observe the deteriorating moral standards of our society as signs that the end is drawing near. Their only hope is that Jesus will get His people out of this collapsing evil world before it is too late.

The message of the Jubilee offers a sharply different perspective on the End Times by examining Bible prophecy in its original Jewish context. The Apostle Peter speaks of the Jubilee as "*the restoration of all things... spoken by mouth of all His holy prophets*" (Acts 3:21).

In this book we are going to discover that the Jubilee is a message of hope in the midst of darkness, of new life out of death, of the wicked being removed from power and the meek inheriting the Kingdom. We will uncover how the Jubilee is the message Jesus proclaimed in His First Coming and is the hope that sustained the early Church through its hardest times of persecution. Finally we will uncover how the Jubilee is at the very core of the good news that will be proclaimed in all the world before Jesus' glorious Return.

Come with me as we begin this exciting journey of discovery.

Ps. Enoch Lavender
Olive Tree Ministries

Updated and Revised Edition

Welcome to the updated and expanded edition of *The Jubilee: Understanding the End Time Mystery*.

In the year that has passed since first publishing this book, I have had the privilege to travel with my wife and family sharing the message of the Jubilee in Churches, seminars and home groups all across the eastern seaboard of Australia. As we minister this message, invariably people come forward for prayer, with many lives touched, healed and transformed through the fresh understanding of God's heart revealed in this book.

This updated and expanded edition features an additional 40 pages of teaching, which has emerged out of further revelation gained on our ministry journeys.

To get the most out of this book, I would recommend reading the chapters sequentially, as each chapter builds on the revelations provided in the prior chapters.

To aid your study, we have included reflection questions at the end of each chapter as well a helpful index of topics.

Like so many others before you, may your life be touched and blessed by the revelations contained in this book, as we together prepare ourselves for the soon Coming of our Lord and King.

Ps Enoch Lavender
Olive Tree Ministries

Jesus and the Jubilee

1

The Jubilee Concept

When God led the people of Israel into the Promised Land, He not only gave the land as a whole as their inheritance, but He also apportioned it individually to tribes, clans and families. The land each Israeli farmer owned was therefore a unique gift and inheritance directly from God Himself.

However, life in the Promised Land was far from easy. Living in such a dry climate, farmers were totally dependent on rain coming in the right season. While God had promised rain as a blessing to those who obeyed Him (see for example Deut. 28:12), far too often the people of Israel turned away from God and began to worship the gods of the surrounding nations. As a result, many farmers were hit hard as drought, plagues and even war ravaged the land.

Through the Law of Moses, God had in advance provided a way to handle such severe financial hardship, allowing Israelites to sell their land to pay off their debts. It is hard to imagine the shame, disappointment and heartbreak such a situation would bring for an Israeli farmer. After all, this was the land God had uniquely given to them and their family. It was His destiny, His plan for them. Yet now, through what often was their own mistakes, they were forced to let go of it and were left to face an uncertain future with their families.

It has been said, "*when it rains, it pours*". In other words, one disaster seldom comes alone. If things went from bad to worse for these poverty-stricken families and their debts continued to rise, the next shameful step was to sell themselves and their families into slavery.

Yet in the midst of this horrible situation, the Scriptures provided a glimmer of hope. The land and the people ultimately both belonged to God (Lev. 25:23,42) and were never to be sold for ever. The land and the people could be "redeemed", i.e. released from slavery and restored to their land, if only a wealthy relative was willing to pay the price.

What if there was no redeemer found? What if there was no "rich uncle" found willing and able to pay the price of this debt? In that case, God Himself would step forward and cancel the debts of His people in the 50th year, known as the Jubilee year.

This once-in-a-generation Jubilee would always be announced with the sounding of the ancient shofar, a trumpet made out of a ram's horn. Can you imagine the joy that would break loose over the entire country of Israel at the sounding of this trumpet? Can you imagine the tears of joy as the slaves were set free across the nation, and as long-lost relatives embraced again? The streets of ancient Israel would have resounded with dancing and shouts of joy with the poor praising God for releasing them from their debts and slavery and letting them return home to their ancient properties. What a day it would be!

Could it be there that there is a link between this ancient sounding of the trumpet, this great and glorious moment of restoration, and the great coming of the Lord? After all, when Jesus spoke of the End Times and its associated "birth pains", He gave us the following words of hope and comfort: "*Now when these things begin to happen, look up and lift up your heads, because your **redemption** draws near.*" (Luke 21:28, emphasis added)

The Hope of A Nation

We will study the links between the Jubilee and the End Times later in this book, but first we need to develop a deeper understanding of the Jubilee expectation surrounding Jesus' 1st Coming.

Looking back at the history of Israel, we see how they quickly turned away from God to worshipping foreign idols. Despite the repeated warnings of the prophets, the measure of sin in the nation continued to build up until they reached the point of moral bankruptcy. Before long, the Northern Tribes of Israel were taken captive and snatched far away from their God-given inheritance, with the Southern Kingdom of Judah soon to follow. The Jewish nation found itself in slavery and in chains, far away from their God-given inheritance, and longing for redemption to occur on a national level. This great restoration of Israel became a central and recurring theme for the prophets of Israel as they looked forward to the coming of the Messiah, the Great Redeemer of His people.

Let's review some key passages from Isaiah for context.

Isaiah's Prophetic Vision

> "Arise, shine;
> For your light has come!
> And the glory of the Lord is risen upon you....
> The Gentiles shall come to your light (Israel)....,
> Your sons shall come from afar (i.e. exile),
> And your daughters shall be nursed at your side....
> And they shall call you The City of the Lord,
> Zion of the Holy One of Israel....
> ... You shall know that I, the Lord, am your Savior
> And your Redeemer..." (Is. 60:1-16)

This prophetic passage from Isaiah is often taught in Churches as applying to Christians, but in its original context the whole chapter is speaking about God restoring Israel, bringing back His glory to her, returning her exiled captives and all this is in the context of God revealing Himself to them as their Redeemer.

How will this beautiful prophecy of Isaiah be fulfilled? Our clue is found in the next chapter, the famous Messianic prophecy of Isaiah 61.

> "The Spirit of the Lord God is upon Me,
> Because the Lord has anointed Me
> To preach good tidings to the poor;
> He has sent Me to heal the brokenhearted,
> To proclaim liberty to the captives,
> And the opening of the prison to *those who are* bound;
> To proclaim the acceptable year of the Lord....
> ...To comfort all who mourn,
> To console those who mourn in Zion
> (Is. 61:1-2)

The Anointed One in this passage is Israel's long-awaited Messiah. But what is the purpose of this Messiah? Isaiah declares that He comes in order to "*proclaim the acceptable year of the Lord*", or more literally "*the year of the Lord's favour / good pleasure*". To understand this concept, we need to see it through the eyes of the Jubilee.

God is really under no obligation to free His people, nor to pay off their debts. He would have been fully within His rights to just let them continue to struggle by themselves. "*It's your debt, you incurred it, so now you pay it yourself*", He could have said. Yet in His favour towards His people, it pleases God in the Jubilee year to pick up and pay the debts they could never pay by themselves. This is truly the year of the Lord's favour on His people. According to Isaiah, the mission of the Messiah is to announce the arrival of this very special year on the calendar and to usher in this amazing time of restoration.

The Messiah is further described by Isaiah as preaching "*good tidings to the poor*". The announcing of the Jubilee would be amazing, life-changing news to the poor, to the bankrupt and those who have lost everything. It would bring comfort to the brokenhearted, "*freedom to the captives*" and the "*opening of the prison*" for those in chains just as Isaiah said. And this great Messianic Jubilee would not just be for individuals but would involve the redemption of the entire nation of Israel as we saw in the previous chapter of Isaiah.

Time to Rebuild

The restoration of God's people to their ancient lands leads naturally to the next step of the prophecy:

> And they shall rebuild the old ruins,
> They shall raise up the former desolations,
> And they shall repair the ruined cities,
> The desolations of many generations.
> (Is. 61:4)

As the Jews return to their ancient properties and take possession of them, they will do what any homeowner would if they were coming back to their former properties. They will proudly pick up their tools and start the hard work necessary to rebuild and restore these properties back to their former glory. After all, this is their inheritance and their God-given possession.

The Day Of Vengeance

> ...And the day of vengeance of our God;....
> (Is. 61:2)

In the midst of this comforting prophetic promise of restoration, we are confronted with the rather frightening concept of the vengeance of God.

In Hebrew, the word 'to redeem' doesn't just mean to pay off a debt, but it also means to 'pay back' or to take righteous revenge on the oppressors of God's people. In Jesus' day there was therefore a strong expectation that the Messiah would not only redeem Israel, but also issue judgment on the Roman occupiers of their land. We will examine how this correlates to the End Times later in this book.

A Messianic Message of Hope

The Jubilee forms an important framework for the Jewish expectation surrounding Jesus' First Coming. Did Jesus fulfil the Jubilee? Did He redeem Israel as promised? Come and find the answer with me as we examine Jesus' message and miracles through the expectation and hope found in the Jubilee.

Reflection Questions
1. How often does the Jubilee occur?
2. How is the Jubilee announced?
3. From what you have learned so far, do you think there is a link between the Jubilee and Jesus' Return? If so, how?

2

The Jubilee Messiah

A woman was once planning a holiday in Switzerland. She was going to rent a small apartment for her stay but couldn't find any information about its toilet. She wrote to the local owner asking about the location of the "WC". Being unfamiliar with this term, the owner thought she was asking about the nearby Wood Chapel and began to describe this wonderful place where people enjoyed congregating together and spending all day together doing sing-alongs!

When reading the Bible, we can sometimes make the same mistake as this property owner, thinking we understand precisely what is written, while actually getting it completely wrong.

> Now after John was put in prison, Jesus came to Galilee, preaching the **gospel of the kingdom of God**
> (Mar. 1:14, emphasis added)

Jesus' ministry and message centred around the "gospel of the kingdom". But what if the word gospel had a fundamentally different meaning in Jesus' day than that used by most Evangelicals today?

Expecting the Redeemer

The Jews were allowed to return to their land during the days of Nehemiah and Ezra, but still found themselves enslaved to cruel and oppressive foreign powers until the time of Jesus' birth. While God had promised Abraham a land stretching "*from the river of Egypt to the great river, the River Euphrates*" (Gen 15:8), under Roman rule the Jews didn't even own a square centimetre of what was promised.

By the time of Jesus' birth, the hope and expectation of the coming Redeemer was sky-high. When Jesus was brought to the Temple to be circumcised as an 8-day old baby, His parents Joseph and Mary encountered the elderly Simeon and Anna. Simeon had spent a lifetime of devotion waiting "*for the restoration of Israel*" (Luke 2:25, Common English Bible)[1] and blessed the Lord for allowing him to see the Child. Anna was likewise thrilled to see Jesus and excitedly spoke of Him to all "*who looked for **redemption** in Jerusalem*" (Luke 2:36, emphasis added).

At thirty years of age, Jesus started His public ministry, with a powerful sermon from the book of Isaiah. "*The Spirit of the Lord is upon me...*" He began, "*to preach good tidings to the poor... liberty to the captives... To proclaim the acceptable year of the Lord... And they shall rebuild the old ruins...*" (Luke 4:17-19).

As this prophecy speaks of the Messiah declaring the Jubilee, it is no wonder that the people in the synagogue were left staring mesmerised at Him (Luke 4:20). Did He mean to say that this was finally the year when their slavery to Rome would be over? Was this finally the time when Israel's freedom would be restored, and their God-given land restored to them as spoken by the prophets? And most importantly, was Jesus the prophesied Redeemer who was going to bring all this to pass?

Preaching the Gospel

> And Jesus went about all Galilee, teaching in their synagogues, preaching the gospel of the kingdom, and healing all kinds of sickness and all kinds of disease among the people.
> (Matt. 4:23)

As Jesus continued His public ministry, His message was described simply as "the gospel of the kingdom". Today, when we hear the word "gospel", we tend to think of the basic message of Christianity; namely that mankind is separated from God through sin and that Jesus paid the penalty for our sin through His death, burial and resurrection. While this is true, there is no record of Jesus directly preaching this message to the crowds.

Besides that, Jesus even sent His disciples out to preach the gospel (Luke 9:6). If Jesus' disciples were listening to Jesus preaching of His coming death, burial and resurrection for the three years of His public ministry, and were themselves also preaching this message, why then were they so confused and depressed after Jesus' crucifixion? Surely they should have known what was coming next? After all, isn't this the crux of the gospel message?

A Closer Look at the Gospel

To resolve this enigma, we must understand that in its original Jewish context, the word gospel already had a meaning. The word "gospel" simply means "good news" and relates directly to the Jubilee as we saw in Isaiah chapter 61.

Jesus' use of the word gospel was therefore not about saving faith in Him (important as it is). Instead, He was proclaiming that the miraculous age of the Jubilee restoration was at hand. The day of redemption, of debt cancellation for the poor, of a new beginning for slaves and the oppressed and for the full restoration of Israel were all implied in this simple phrase found at the very core of His message.

Not only did Jesus proclaim the Jubilee, but as we will discover in our next chapter, His miracles testified of it's coming as well. As we study these miraculous signs, we will catch glimpses of what the great and final Jubilee will look like and discover why Peter calls it "*the time of restoration of all things*". (Acts 3:21) Just as the ancient Israelites looked forward to the coming of the Jubilee, so this final fulfilment of its prophetic promise will be something to look forward to.

---

[1] Other versions translate this particular phrase as 'the comfort / consolation of Israel'.

Reflection Questions
1. How does the word 'gospel' relate to the Jubilee?
2. Why were the disciples so confused when Jesus died?
3. Jesus was announcing and preaching the Jubilee, but in what ways did He fulfil it?
4. What aspects of the Jubilee did Jesus not fulfil?

3

The Miracles of the Jubilee

Moving house can be a messy and frantic nightmare for even the most organised couples. The first time my wife and I moved house, we thought we had the perfectly organised system. We carefully placed all our belongings into boxes and marked each box with a number. We meticulously made an inventory of our packed items in numbered boxes. It was going to be a fool proof system, or so we thought.

When we arrived at our new home and started unpacking, we realised we had made a big mistake. We had packed the inventory list inside one of the boxes and had no idea where it was! While we could clearly see the numbers on each box, without our list we were helplessly unable to decipher what they meant.

The Bible describes Jesus' many miracles as signs. This means that they carry a meaning to be understood, much like the numbers on our packing boxes. In order to decipher the message of Jesus' miracles, we need to look back to the context of Old Testament prophecy.

After all, this was the Bible of the early Apostles and the Jewish community in their day. This was the God-given standard to which any prophet would be measured and through which their ministry would be understood. By the age of 13, many young Jewish boys in Jesus' day would have memorised the entire Old Testament[1]. They would have been intimately familiar with the words of the prophets and in them would have seen a deeper meaning and promise to Jesus' many miracles. What then was the message of Jesus' miracles, and did it have any connection to the long-awaited Jubilee?

Jesus' First Sign

> And when they ran out of wine, the mother of Jesus said to Him, "They have no wine." ...This beginning of signs Jesus did in Cana of Galilee, and manifested His glory; and His disciples believed in Him.
> (John 2:3,11)

If you were Jesus, what would you choose as your first miracle? Turning water into wine was certainly not a sign I would have picked!

Yet for Jews intimately familiar with the Old Testament, this sign would naturally have turned their attention to the prophets Joel and Micah. Both of these prophets speak of the future return of the Jews to their land (i.e the Jubilee) in connection with a miraculous abundance of wine:

> "For behold, in those days and at that time,
> **When I bring back the captives** of Judah and Jerusalem...
> .... [18] And it will come to pass in that day
> That the **mountains shall drip with new wine,**
> (Joel 3:1, 18, emphasis added)

> "Behold, the days are coming," says the Lord,
> "When the **plowman shall overtake the reaper**,
> And the treader of grapes him who sows seed;
> The **mountains shall drip with sweet wine**,
> And all the hills shall flow with it.
> **I will bring back the captives** of My people Israel;
> They shall **build the waste cities** and inhabit them;
> They shall **plant vineyards** and **drink wine** from them....
> (Amos 9:13-14)

These prophecies link the prophesied Jewish return to their ancient homeland, with the farms of Israel literally overflowing with God's blessings of wine and the best produce. While Christians throughout history have taught 'deeper' spiritual meaning to such prophecies, the Jews in Jesus' day would have fully expected both a literal re-possessing of their ancient homeland as well as a real physical abundance to follow. After all, the Law of Moses had promised God's abundant provision for Israel in the Land (i.e. Deut. 28).

The Rabbis say that to this day, Israel has never experienced the full manifestation of these blessings. Yet in Israel's great day of restoration, when the Lord Himself redeems His people and pays their debt, then these blessings will be released in their full manifestation.

Abundance of Food

The New Testament tells us the story of how Jesus took a young boy's lunch, consisting of five loaves and two small fish, and multiplied the food to feed a crowd of over 5'000 men plus women and children (John 6:1-14). However, there was more to this miracle than simply meeting the crowd's temporary needs or demonstrating Jesus' divine power. To the Jews conversant in the Hebrew Scriptures, this would have brought to mind Jeremiah's prophecies of the coming redemption:

> 'He who scattered Israel will gather him.....'
> For the Lord has **redeemed** Jacob,
> And **ransomed** him from the hand of one stronger than he.
> Therefore they shall come and sing in the height of Zion,
> Streaming to the **goodness** of the Lord-
> For **wheat** and **new wine** and **oil**,
> For the **young of the flock** and the herd;
> Their souls shall be like a well-watered garden,
> And they shall sorrow no more at all.
> (Jer 31:10-12, emphasis added)

The Deaf Hear, the Blind See and the Lame Walk

Jesus' public ministry was characterised by a steady stream of healings and miracles. This too was beautifully foretold by the prophets:

> Then the **eyes of the blind** shall be opened,
> And the **ears of the deaf** shall be unstopped.
> Then the **lame shall leap** like a deer,
> And the tongue of **the dumb sing**.
> (Is. 35:5-6, emphasis added)

It is important to be aware that this prophecy from Isaiah speaks of these miracles in the context of the Jubilee when "*the ransomed of the Lord shall return, And come to Zion with singing*" (v. 10).

But why would physical healing be linked to the day of redemption? One way to understand this is that our physical bodies and even life itself is a gift, a divine inheritance from God given to each of us.

However, through our sins and the sins of those around us, the enemy finds a way in and begins to oppress this God-given inheritance. Yet in the Jubilee, God is our redeemer, freeing us from the debt of sin and bringing health, healing and restoration to our physical bodies.

The Scriptures describe God redeeming Israel from Egypt, bringing them out of slavery to take them to the Promised Land of their inheritance. And when He brought them out, "*there was none feeble among [them]*" (Ps. 105:37). In other words, as the redemption took effect, there was an instant mass healing of the Jews departing the bondage of Egypt. How much more then will the future redemption not only includes Israel being restored to her land, but also include a dramatic wave of healings and restoration of physical bodies as spoken by Isaiah? Maybe this is the reason why Paul says that we "*groan within ourselves, eagerly waiting for... the redemption of our body*" (Rom. 8:23)?

Each miracle Jesus performed was a sign building the expectation that the Jubilee Age was imminent. Yet there was an even greater sign to come, which would send Jesus' Jewish crowd rapturous with excitement.

Lazarus Reveals God's Glory

Towards the end of Jesus' earthly ministry, tragedy struck as His close friend Lazarus died. By the time Jesus arrived, he had already been in the tomb for four days. Lazarus' sister Martha came running to Jesus and tearfully exclaimed "*Lord, if You had been here, my brother would not have died*" (John 6:21)

In the ensuing conversation, Martha spoke of her faith that Lazarus will rise "*in the resurrection at the last day*" (v. 24). In other words, her hope is to one day see Lazarus raised physically back to life here on earth. Acknowledging the truth of Martha's words, Jesus replied that He is "'*he resurrection and the life*" (v. 25) as He headed to the tomb. There in plain sight of the crowd who had gathered to weep, Jesus commanded Lazarus to "*come forth*". Suddenly, this man who had been dead for four days emerged alive out of the tomb!

This spectacular miracle was seen as a tremendous sign of the coming redemption through Jesus as the Messiah.

Is there a link between the resurrection and the Jubilee? We will examine this later in the book, but for now, think of it this way; the dead have lost everything. Through the curse of sin they have lost their health, their wealth, their family and their land. It has all gone, and they are totally powerless to redeem themselves or bring it back. But the Bible promises that one day the dead will physically rise again ushering in the greatest day of restoration the world has ever seen.

Bearing this in mind, it is no wonder that the Jews who saw the miracle of Lazarus' resurrection, excitedly spread the word everywhere. As a result, only a few days later an exuberant crowd welcomed Jesus to Jerusalem with the Messianic cry "*Blessed is He who comes in the Name of the Lord*" (see John 12:12-13, 17-18). With the Messianic fervour reaching fever pitch in Jerusalem, the Pharisees were left gloomily saying to each other "*Look the whole world has gone after him*" (John 12:19).

It appeared to the disciples and most of Jerusalem that they were on the very cusp of the Jubilee. They had heard Jesus' first sermon declaring the Jubilee, they had seen the Messianic signs Jesus had displayed, they had tasted of the abundance of wine and food, they had seen the healing of the deaf, blind and lame and now the raising of the dead. It was obvious in their minds that now was the time when it would all be released in its fullness as Jesus entered the Holy City of Jerusalem.

Yet only a few days later, their dreams and hopes would come crashing down at the skull shaped hill of Golgotha.

---

[1] Greenwold, Doug. *Reflections, A Digging Deeper Faith Study*

Reflection Questions

1. Understanding that Jesus' many miracles were signs, what was the message they conveyed?
2. Describe in your own words the miracles we will see in the great future Messianic Jubilee.
3. Why did Jesus announce the Jubilee at the beginning of His ministry if He didn't fulfil it?

4

The Hope of Redemption

Only a few days after Jesus' triumphal entry to Jerusalem, the people's expectant hope of an imminent Jubilee came crashing down. Jesus was betrayed by one of his own, handed over to the Romans by the chief priests and nailed to the cross like a common criminal. As Jesus' breathed His last, the hope of the Redemption of Israel appeared to be all but over. Having invested three years of their life to following Jesus, leaving everything and everyone else behind; Jesus' disciples must have felt totally crushed.

Two of the disciples spoke frankly of their deep disillusionment a few days later as they were travelling to Emmaus. You can hear the disappointment in their voices as they told the stranger travelling with them that they thought *"Jesus of Nazareth... was He who was going to redeem Israel"* (Luke 24:19-21). We can only imagine their surprise soon after when they discovered that the stranger was the resurrected Jesus!

Encountering the risen Lord must have brought great comfort to the bewildered disciples. Jesus spent the next 40 days with them, teaching them about the Kingdom. At their first opportunity, the disciples asked Jesus a question that must have been burning on their hearts. *"Lord will you at this time restore the kingdom to Israel?"* (Acts 1:6). In other words, after everything that has happened, is the Jubilee next on the agenda?

Some modern theologians have condemned the disciples at this point, claiming that they *"still don't get it"*. They insist the disciples are still distracted from the mission of Jesus and are instead focused on Israel's physical kingdom. But in light of the Jubilee, I believe the disciples knew full well what they were asking. They knew this was the message of the prophets, they knew that Jesus had announced the Jubilee in His very first sermon, and that all His miracles were signs pointing to the Jubilee, with the resurrection being the greatest of them all. Why would Jesus do these things if He wasn't going to bring the Jubilee? Surely the time was now?

Rather than dismissing their question, Jesus said it was not for them to know the *"times or seasons which the Father has put in His own authority"* (v.7). In other words, the Jubilee is still coming, but the disciples must for now focus their attention on being Jesus' witnesses *"to the ends of the earth"* (v.8)

Shortly after this conversation, Jesus ascended to Heaven and the disciples obediently returned to Jerusalem. A few days after the outpouring of the Holy Spirit on Pentecost, the newly empowered Peter and John encounter a lame man in the Temple begging for alms. *"Silver and gold I do not have"* Peter stated, *"but what I do have I give you: In the name of Jesus Christ of Nazareth, rise up and walk."* (Acts. 3:6)

Instantly the lame man rises from his bed and an amazed crowd gathers to watch the commotion. Under the inspiration of the Holy Spirit, Peter addressed the crowd. Jesus **"has to remain** in heaven", Peter explains, "until the **time comes for restoring everything**, as God said long ago... through the holy prophets" (Acts 3:21, CJB emphasis added). Let's first note how Peter calls the Jubilee the *"time of the restoration of all things"*. In light of what we have learned, this very accurately describes the essence of the Jubilee.

Peter strongly states that Jesus cannot return *until* this time of restoration. In other words, Jesus' return is inextricably linked to the Jubilee, and He simply cannot return until it is time for that great final Jubilee to be fulfilled.

According to Peter, this restoration and its links to the Messiah's coming has been spoken of by all the prophets. For years, I personally struggled with this Scripture. "*Where do the prophets speak of this?*", I asked myself as I searched in vain for references to the "*restoration of all things*" in the Old Testament. While this exact phrase does not occur in the Old Testament, my study of the Jubilee has helped me realise that it the "restoration of all things" is indeed central to the message of the prophets.

The Hope of Jesus' Return

When Jesus Himself spoke of the End Times, He foretold many great and terrifying calamaties. "*Nation will rise against nation*", and in that terrible time there will be "*famines, pestilences and earthquakes*" accompanied by great persecution and deception (Matt 24:4-11). In the midst of this onslaugt of evil, Jesus gives us an amazing statement of hope:

> Now when these things begin to happen, look up and lift
> up your heads, because your **redemption** draws near.
> (Luke 21:28, emphasis added)

Because we as a Church have not understood the Jubilee concept, we have struggled to understand what this future redemption is all about. "*Didn't Jesus already redeem us on the cross?*", we may ask. And when we don't understand this hope of redemption, all that is left are Jesus' dire warnings of the troubles surrounding the End of Days. As a result many in the Church have been left with a very negative perception of the End Times.

I firmly believe God wants His people to re-discover the hope of Jesus' return, and to carry the same excitement and anticipation that ancient Israel would have felt towards the Jubilee. They were excitedly waiting for that trumpet to sound, and may we too wait for that Day with great joy!

In our next chapters we will explore in detail the exciting theme of the links between Jesus' return and the final Jubilee.

Reflection Questions
1. Why were the disciples so crushed by the death of Jesus?
2. According to Peter, when will the Jubilee come?
3. What is the hope Jesus offer us to hold on to during the hard times before His return?

The End Times
and the Jubilee

5

The Trumpet of Mt. Sinai

It was possibly the most dramatic moment in all of Israel's history. The tribes of Israel had gathered at the foot of Mount Sinai after their dramatic escape from captivity to Pharoah. The awesome miracles of Egypt, including the crossing of the Red Sea, were all about to pale into insignificance.

What was about to occur was a manifestation of the God of the universe in a way never seen before or since in world history. God Himself was about to physically descend on Mount Sinai in the sight of all the people. Many theologians agree that this whole event was a majestic preview of what is to come when Jesus returns in glory.

Did the Mount Sinai event also include links to the Jubilee, and if so, what does it tell us about the connection between the Jubilee and the return of Jesus?

An Encounter on the Mountain

Fifty days after they left Egypt[1], the moment had finally come for the Israelites to approach Mount Sinai. As the twelve tribes looked up, they saw the top of Mount Sinai being enveloped in a thick cloud. Suddenly thunder and lightning erupted from the cloud. The awestruck Israelites were awestruck as the entire mountain erupted in smoke and shaking as the Lord Himself physically descended upon its peak.

An exceedingly loud and long trumpet blast resounded through the air. The Bible doesn't reveal who sounded the trumpet, could it have been an angel or God Himself?

> When the **trumpet** (yobel) sounds long, they shall come near the mountain..... And when the blast of the trumpet sounded long and became louder and louder, Moses spoke, and God answered him by voice. Then the Lord came down upon Mount Sinai....
> (Ex 19:13, 16-20, emphasis added)

The normal Hebrew word for trumpet is "*shofar*", but in verse 13 we are surprised to find the word "*yobel*" normally translated Jubilee. Why is the Jubilee mentioned in this context? Could there be a link between this event and the Jubilee? After all, the Jubilee is always announced with sounding of the trumpet:

> Then you shall cause the **trumpet of the Jubilee** to sound on the tenth day of the seventh month
> (Lev 25:9, emphasis added)

At Mount Sinai, Israel was truly in the midst of her own Jubilee experience, having been released from slavery to inherit their promised land. But could there be more to the Mount Sinai story? Is there also a future significance, linking this dramatic encounter with God, to His Return and the beginning of the Jubilee?

The Trumpet of God

Following the pattern of Mt. Sinai, Jesus will one day descend from Heaven in awesome glory, and it is certainly no co-incidence that it too will be marked with the sounding of a great heavenly trumpet blast.

In the words of Paul the Apostle:

> For the Lord Himself will descend from heaven with a shout, with the voice of an archangel, and with the **trumpet of God**. And the dead in Christ will rise first. Then we who are alive and remain shall be caught up together with them in the clouds to meet the Lord in the air. And thus we shall always be with the Lord.
> (I Thes 4:16-17, emphasis added)

The trumpet involved in the Return of Jesus will not simply be a dramatic background noise. The Mount Sinai experience indcates that it will also simultaneously be a Jubilee trumpet, announcing what Peter describes as *'the time of the restoration of all things'* (Acts. 3:21).

The triumphant chorus of the praise song *'Days of Elijah'* captures this moment well:

> "Behold He comes riding on the clouds,
> Shining like the sun at **the trumpet call**,
> Lift your voice, it's the **year of jubilee**,
> And out of Zion's hill salvation comes."

In our next chapter we are going to begin to look at the Resurrection of the Dead and how it plays a crucial role in the promised restoration of all things. The finality of death, and the great loss we all feel at the graves of our loved ones, will one day be turned around to great joy. What a day of restoration that will be!

---

[1] According to Jewish traditional counting, it was 50 days after Passover, at the feast of Pentecost (which means 50), that the glory of God was revealed at Mount Sinai. Interestingly, the number 50 is linked to both this encounter and to the Jubilee itself.

Reflection Questions

1. What is the normal Hebrew word for trumpet?
2. Why was the Hebrew word "yobel" or Jubilee used in the Exodus 19 passage?
3. If the Mount Sinai experience was prophetic of Jesus' Second Coming, what does it teach us about getting ready for that day? (see Ex. 19:10-15)

6

Introducing The Resurrection

A highlight of any Christian tour to Israel includes a stop at the majestic Mount of Olives. This site gives an uninterrupted panoramic view of the Old City of Jerusalem. It was from here that Jesus ascended to Heaven, and it also marks the spot where He will one day return (Acts 1:9-12 compare Zec. 14:4).

An unexpected sight awaiting Mount Olive's pilgrims, is the large number of mostly Jewish graves covering its gentle slopes. The Mount of Olives is in fact one of the largest and most important Jewish grave sites in the world holding up to 150,000 tombs. These graves lie as a silent testament to the Jewish belief in the Resurrection of the Dead, and the belief that the Resurrection will start right here on the Mount of Olives[1].

The Resurrection and Jesus' Return

The Resurrection of the Dead is a central feature of Jesus' return:

> For the **trumpet will sound**, and **the dead will be raised** incorruptible, and we shall be changed.
> (I Cor 15:52, emphasis added)

> For the Lord Himself will descend from heaven with a shout, with the voice of an archangel, and **with the trumpet of God**. And the **dead in Christ will rise** first.
> (1 Thes. 4:16, emphasis added)

Both our Corinthian and Thessalonian passages agree: the first thing that happens as the Jubilee trumpet announces the Return of Jesus is the raising up of the dead.

The Resurrection of the Dead will be the single greatest event of restoration to occur in the history of mankind. After all, when you are dead, you have lost everything, your life, health, wealth and family. But as the Jubilee trumpet of restoration sounds, millions of dead all over this planet will be restored to life in renewed bodies.

Belief in the Resurrection is foundational to understanding the coming Jubilee. However, this belief clashes sharply with the ancient teachings of the Gnostics, which not only influenced the early Church but still echo through the corridors of Christian theology down to this day. In this chapter we are going to start peeling away layers of Gnosticism as we seek to understand the great promise of the Jubilee and the Resurrection in its original Biblical context.

The Teachings of Gnostism

In theory, mainstream Christian Churches all embrace the doctrine of the Resurrection of the Dead. However, in practice, many Christians have their understanding of the afterlife clouded with the teachings of Plato and the Gnostics.

Plato, who lived in the 4th Century BC, famously taught that the material world is just an illusion like the flickering of shadows on the walls of a cave. He taught that the goal of life was to get in touch with the true realities beyond this physical world.

Plato's teachings were the fundamental inspiration of the Gnostics who later infiltrated the ranks of the early first century Church. They taught that we are made for a world without space, time and matter, a place of pure spiritual existence[2]. This way of thinking influenced early Christianity to the point that many ended up devaluing the body and this planet, seeking only to escape to the spiritual safety of Heaven.

It was with this mindset that the Greek scholars in Athens had no qualms listening to the Apostle Paul proclaiming the story of Jesus and His many miracles. They also had no real misgivings about Jesus being the Son of God. After all they already had many gods and could easily add another to their pantheon. But when Paul began to speak of the Resurrection, the crowd reacted strongly. As described in the Message translation "*At the phrase "raising him from the dead," the listeners split: Some laughed at him and walked off making jokes; others said, "Let's do this again. We want to hear more."* " (Acts 17:32, MSG)

The Kingdom of Heaven

For Gnostics, Heaven is seen as the perfect destination to escape this material world. The Gnostic perspective easily misunderstands the gospel writer Matthew's many references to Heaven. Let's look at just a few examples:

> Blessed are the poor in spirit, For theirs is the kingdom of Heaven.
> (Matt. 5:3)
> Blessed are those who are persecuted for righteousness' sake, For theirs is the kingdom of Heaven.
> (Matt. 5:10)
> Not everyone who says to Me, 'Lord, Lord,' shall enter the kingdom of Heaven, but he who does the will of My Father in heaven.
> (Matt. 7:21)

At first glance it appears that these Scriptures are showing how it should be our ambition and goal to end up in a spiritual place called Heaven. However, a closer look at the Jewish context begins to reveal a different understanding.

The Torah[3] specifically forbade the Jews from taking "*God's name in vain*" (Ex. 20:7). Therefore, Matthew followed the common custom of his day by swapping out references to God's Name with the word heaven. Today people similarly use the phrase '*Oh for Heaven's Sake*" instead of offensively using God's Name.

Matthew's many references to the "*Kingdom of Heaven*" were simply referring to the same entity Luke described in his gospel as "*the Kingdom of God*". This kingdom was expected to be a literal reign coming soon to planet Earth. Jesus' teaching in these verses was therefore not about the conditions of entry required for a spiritual home in Heaven, but rather about how to enter the future Kingdom of the Messiah here on Earth. The Jewish context therefore reveals a radically different perspective on Jesus' words than that held by Gnosticism.

Echoes of Gnosticism

The influence of the early Gnostics have echoed their way down through the centuries of Christian tradition and can be heard to this day in Christian sermons and worship songs.

Take for example these sayings:

> "Earth is Heaven's waiting room"
> "We don't belong to this planet; Heaven is our true home"
> "The real you is on the inside"
> "Life on earth is like a pregnancy, getting you ready for a new and very different life in eternity"

For many Christians these statements are seen as gospel truth. But these statements lie at the heart of the conflict between Gnosticism and the Biblical belief in the Resurrection and even undermines the purpose of the Jubilee.

If Earth is merely Heaven's waiting room, why should God restore this planet? And if Heaven is our home, why would He restore Israel to their ancient homeland? And if the real us is the person on the inside, why would God raise the dead physically to life?

If we are to grasp the purpose of the Jubilee restoration here on Earth, we need to start by recapturing the first century belief in the Resurrection as taught and demonstrated by Jesus and His followers. Let's begin our journey of understanding by turning to the story of Jesus and his close friends Mary, Martha and Lazarus.

[1] *Mount of Olives Jewish Cemetery*, Wikipedia, https://en.wikipedia.org/wiki/Mount_of_Olives_Jewish_Cemetery (accessed 14th of August, 2023)

[2] See Tom Wright, *Surprised by Hope* (SPCK, London: 2011), 100-101. See also *Platonism,* https://en.wikipedia.org/wiki/Platonism (accessed July 13, 2023)

[3] Also known as the first five books of the Bible, Genesis to Deuteronomy

Reflection Questions
1. What is Gnosticism?
2. Why does the phrase "Kingdom of Heaven" refer to a literal kingdom of the Messiah here on earth?
3. In what ways is Gnosticism incompatible with the Jubilee?

7

Martha's Hope

Now Martha said to Jesus, "Lord, if You had been here, my brother would not have died. [22] But even now I know that whatever You ask of God, God will give You."
(John 11:21-22)

The scene was one of heartbreak and sadness. Mary and Martha were surrounded by friends and relatives as they grieved the recent loss of their beloved brother Lazarus. They had requested Jesus to come urgently, but now it was too late.

If a modern-day pastor had been in Jesus' shoes you could expect him or her to issue words of comfort centered around the themes of Heaven and eternity.

A modern version of the conversation could have looked something like this:

> The pastor said to her, "You will see your brother again in eternity."
>
> Martha said to the pastor, "I know that I will see him in Heaven."
>
> The pastor said to her, "Jesus is the way to Heaven...."

However, Jesus' conversation with Martha was radically different in focus:

> Jesus said to her, "Your brother will **rise again**."
>
> Martha said to Him, "I know that he will **rise again** in the **resurrection** at the last day."
>
> Jesus said to her, "I am the **resurrection** and the life...
> (John 11:23-25, emphasis added)

This intimate conversation between Jesus and Martha reveals much about the first century Jewish understanding of the afterlife; an understanding which Jesus did not contradict. When facing the loss of her brother, Martha's source of comfort and hope was not on seeing him in Heaven, but rather of one day meeting him again physically here on Earth in '*the Resurrection at the Last Day*'.

The Afterlife

This is not to say that there is no afterlife. With one of His final breaths, Jesus turned to the dying criminal hanging on a cross beside Him, promising him that "*today you will be with me in Paradise*" (Luke 23:43).

Another example is Jesus' story of the beggar Lazarus and the rich man. The story follows the rich man after his death, revealing his torment in the afterlife, in contrast to the comfort received by Lazarus. This powerful story of Jesus shows that in the afterlife the rich man was conscious of his past, was able to recognise and communicate with others in the realm of the dead and was concerned about people back on Earth (Luke 16:19-31).

However, the afterlife was seen as only a temporary place for the dead while awaiting the resurrection[1].

Awaking from Sleep

A helpful metaphore in understanding the difference between the afterlife and the resurrection is found in the Biblical concept of sleep and death. Being dead is often referred to as being 'asleep' in the Bible (see for example 1. Kings 2:10, 11:43, 14:20, 16:6). We even see this in the story of Martha's brother Lazarus:

> .... [Jesus] said to them, "Our friend Lazarus sleeps, but I go that I may wake him up."
> (John 11:11)

Like the afterlife, sleep is a state of rest where one is out of touch with the physical surroundings of Earth. The afterlife, like sleep, is only temporary, until the time when one wakes up. Just as the clanging sound of an alarm clock wakes us up, so one day the piercing sound of the trumpet will wake us all up from the sleep of death.

Daniel the prophet speaks clearly of this:

> And many of those who sleep in the dust of the earth shall awake, Some to everlasting life, Some to shame and everlasting contempt.
> (Dan. 12:2)

While sleep is a part of life, our real focus is on the action that happens while we are awake. In the same way, first century Jews such as Martha, were not primarily focused on the sleep of the afterlife, but rather on the awakening to come at the great Resurrection. This was their source of comfort, this was their future hope.

Waking up in our Resurrection Bodies

When we wake up from the sleep of death, we will find ourselves in what we can best describe as upgraded versions of our former bodies (1 Cor. 15:42-44). What will this resurrection body look like?

The Apostle John writes:

> "*when He is revealed, we shall be like Him for we shall see Him as He is.*"
> (1 John 3:2)

Paul the Apostle similarly declares that Jesus is the '*first fruits of those who have fallen asleep*' (1 Cor. 15:20). In other words, Jesus' resurrection body is the prototype, the example giving us a preview of our future resurrection bodies.

What was Jesus' resurrected body like? We note firstly that His body remained recognizable, but at the same time it was also different enough for His disciples to not immediately recognize Him. Secondly, it is important to note that he had a real physical body that could be touched. While He was able to walk through walls and closed doors, Jesus made a point of eating normal food with His disciples to demonstrate that he was not simply a spirit being (Luke 24:39-43). Thirdly, while Jesus' resurrection body still bore the scars of His suffering (John 20:27), all the pain and the destruction His body had suffered no longer affected Him. He was fully healed and restored.

I believe we can expect these same features in our own future resurrection bodies.

The Resurrection and the Jubilee

In Jubilee terms, God has given us all individually the gift of life. It is our inheritance from Him, a precious gift of which our bodies form an important part. But one day, because of our sins and the sins of our forefathers, we will lose our lives and be separated from our bodies as if we were sent into exile. In the Jubilee, when God restores all things and brings His people back to their inheritance, then we too will be restored to life, returning from exile so to speak into our restored human bodies.

Becoming Fearless

Humanity's number one fear is death. As a result, it is normal for people to desperately hold on to life, being willing to almost do anything if it means keeping their lives. But faithful believers in Bible times knew that death was not the end. They knew that one day their lives and everything God had for them would be restored. Here are some amazing examples of how faith in the Resurrection specifically inspired believers both before and after Christ.

Around 167 BC, a horrific wave of persecution engulfed the entire land of Israel. Anyone caught keeping the ways of God would be horrifically tortured and publicly executed under the sinister rule of Antiochus Epiphanes IV. One notable story from this time is that of Hannah and her seven sons who were dragged before the wicked ruler for their commitment to God. Antiochus challenged each one of her sons individually to abandon the God of their forefathers, offering them great and enticing rewards. One by one the sons refused. Instead, they willing presented their bodies to torture and death, while publicly proclaiming their faith in the Resurrection as well as in the coming judgment of the wicked ruler. When he was about to lose his hands, one of the sons said *"God gave these to me. But His laws mean more to me than my hands, and I know God will give them back to me again."* (2 Macc. 7:11, GNT). The turn finally came to the youngest of the sons. In her last words to him, the mother encouraged her son to also be faithful unto death *"so that by God's mercy I may receive you back with them at the resurrection."* (2 Macc. 7:29, GNT)[2].

After the ministry of Jesus and the advent of the Church, it didn't take long before faithful believers again encountered severe persecution. History records a barbaric wave of persecution in Lyons, France. No matter how harshly the Romans persecuted the Church, these early believers refused to give up their faith in Jesus. One day, the Romans discovered their secret. It was the belief in a physical resurrection which motivated these early believers to stand firm.

In response, the Romans came up with a sinister plan to crush this hope once and for all. The plan involved taking the bodies of believers whom they had killed and burning them in the fire until only ashes was left. Roman soldiers then scattered the ashes into a fast-flowing river, hoping that this would render the Resurrection impossible and crush their faith[3]. Thankfully, the Roman plan failed miserably. These faithful believers were not intimidated, but rather had faith that God could even restore life out of these scattered ashes. Like the herioc Jews during the reign of Antiochus, these Christians knew that no matter what the Roman soldiers attempted to take from them, even to the point of life itself, God would one day restore it to them in the Resurrection here on Earth. This is the power of the message of the Resurrection and it is sorely needed in today's Church.

Recapturing the Hope

I have never thought of myself as a particularly brave person (in fact I'm still scared of needles!), but I always find it inspiring to read about these martyrs of the faith. I believe the message of their bravery and of the hope that motivated them is essential reading for us as Christians today.

Jesus specifically warned His followers that dark days of persecution will return with a vengeance in the End Times:

Then they will deliver you up to tribulation and kill you, and you will be hated by all nations for My name's sake.
(Matt 24:9)

Just as the hope of the Resurrection enabled faithful Jews and Christians to stand firm in those dark times, so it's motivating hope can immunize us today from satan's intimidating threats. If he threatens to take our property and wealth away, then we know that God will one day restore it. If he threatens to destroy and kill our bodies, then we know that we have an upgraded body to enjoy in our new life here on Earth. The god of this world can at best only take things away from us temporarily, until the Jubilee comes when it will all be restored by our great Redeemer. This hope sustained the early believers during the darkest of days, and recapturing this hope today will better equip us to face future waves of persecution.

The apostle Paul speaks beautifully of how the hope of the Resurrection motivated him in the midst of the intense persecution he faced:

> **We are hard-pressed** on every side, yet not crushed; we are perplexed, but not in despair; **persecuted, but not forsaken**; struck down, but not destroyed.... **knowing that He who raised up the Lord Jesus will also raise us up with Jesus**, and will present us with you..... Therefore we do not lose heart ....For our light affliction, which is but for a moment, is working for us a far more exceeding and eternal weight of glory
> (2 Cor 4:8-18, emphasis added)

In summary, Martha's hope, and that of the first century believers, was in the coming Resurrection here on Earth. As we embrace this understanding, it will help us put modern day threats of persecution into their proper perspective. Persecution is at its worst only temporary, light 'afflictions', hardly worth mentioning compared to glory of what and Who is soon to come. Amen!

[1] Jesus spoke about their being 'many dwelling places' in His Father's house (John 14:1-2), i.e., in the afterlife. While the English translation may imply a permanent living place, the original word in ancient Greek to refers to a temporary stop on the way to your final destination. See Wright, Surprised by Hope, p. 162

[2] Antiochus Epiphanes IV is described by many theologians as the foremost precursor to the antichrist seen throughout Bible history. For a thorough explanation of this time in history and the prophetic example it sets for the End Times, see my book "Rebuilding the Temple, Preparing for the Lord's Return" available via Amazon and Christian retailers.

[3] Wright, Tom, *Surprised by Hope,* p. 176. See also Sanidopoulos, John, *Holy Martyrs Killed in the Persecution in Lyon in 177 A.D,* June 2, 2019. https://www.johnsanidopoulos.com/2019/06/holy-martyrs-killed-in-persecution-in.html (accessed Aug. 19th, 2023)

Reflection Questions
1. What was Martha's hope concerning Lazarus?
2. What will our resurrection bodies look like?
3. How does faith in the resurrection enable us to face persecution?

8

The Final Victory

> ...on this rock I will build My church, and the gates of Hades shall not prevail against it.
> (Matt. 16:18)

When studied closely, this much quoted saying by Jesus is highly confusing. Hades is commonly understood to refer to Hell, but why would its gates be fighting against the Church? Does it mean that the Church is seeking to break into Hell itself? The Bible teaching ministry *First Fruits of Zion* points out that this much quoted saying by Jesus is in fact a reference to the Saints' future victory over death[1]. They helpfully explain that the word 'Hades' is a translation of the Hebrew term 'Sheol' which refers to the afterlife. The gates of Sheol are defensive structures intended to prevent the dead from passing back to life. However, Jesus promises that these gates will not be able to hold back His Church on the great Day of the Resurrection.

On that day, the gates of Hades will fling wide open as the Saints return to their ancient inheritance. In that great day of rejoicing and jubilation, the believers will rise anew in recreated bodies, physically embracing long lost loved ones with tearful shouts of joy[2].

The revelation of the Resurrection is a great source of comfort when dealing with the loss of a loved one. A few years ago, my family and I discovered this truth for ourselves in a deeply personal way.

Finding Comfort in the Resurrection

> ... the Lord has anointed Me ....to proclaim liberty to the captives [*of death*], ...To comfort all who mourn, ... To give them beauty for ashes, The oil of joy for mourning.
> (Is. 61:1-3, author's comment inserted)

Just over a year and a half had passed since the birth of our twins, and my wife had just become pregnant again. As we began to pray about this new addition to our family, we felt that the Lord give us a name for her, calling her Joy. It was a beautiful name, and we were looking forward to meeting her, having received prophetic words about this little baby.

Very early in the pregnancy, my wife had a small bleed during a time of travelling. The doctors re-assured us that it was nothing to worry about, but told us to get it checked out when she came home. When she went to the check up a few days later, the medical staff soon realised someting had gone terribly wrong. They tried again and again to find baby Joy's heartbeat, but it was in vain. Our little Joy had gone.

As for any couple going through a miscarriage, we were stunned and devastated by the news. The hardest part for me personally was the sense that God had given us clear prophetic words about this little one, and now those words were quite literally falling to the ground unfulfilled. "What kind of 'joy' is this?" I asked myself, "Did I get it wrong? Why has this happened to us?"

During my personal devotion times in the days leading up to the miscarriage, I had "happened" to study the topic of the Resurrection. As I reflected back on what had happened, I soon began to find great comfort in the Resurrection. I considered the many unfulfilled prophecies given to Israel and realised that while these promises seem impossible to fulfil right now, God is faithful to His Word and will fulfil them in the coming Jubilee Age.

I came to understand that these are not the only promises that will await fulfilment in the Messianic Age. God's promises to us concerning our little baby Joy will also come to pass in that great day of restoration. We will not just one day meet her again in spiritually in heaven. There is coming a day when our little baby will physically and literally rise from the grave. And on that day, my wife and I will be there. With tears and shouts of joy we will run to embrace her, giving her a hug for the very first time. Oh what Joy it will be!

And that great day will not only be our day of joy, but that of millions of others as well as they hug and embrace their resurrected loved ones here on earth. This will truly be the greatest moment of restoration the world have ever seen, and it will happen at the jubilee trumpet. As Paul says "*the trumpet will sound, and the dead will be raised*" (1 Cor. 15:52). And on that day, the prophetic meaning of our baby girl's name will be fulfilled, as it will truly be the day of greatest joy ever known to the history of the world. What a day to finally encounter our Joy!

Dealing with Grief

We have all experienced grief and sadness over the loss of a loved one. It may have been unexpected and sudden, through a long and trying battle with illness, or simply the result of old age. Whatever the cause, the grief and sorrow is a very real and heavy burden to bear.

My prayer is that our personal story of loss and of the hope we have found in the Resurrection will also minister comfort to you.

As we close this chapter and of our teaching on the Resurrection, may I take a moment to pray for you?

Dear Heavenly Father,

I thank you for each of my readers right now.

I ask you to minister by Your Holy Spirit to the hearts of those who still carry grief over the loss of loved ones.

Together with them, I acknowledge the pain and grief they have experienced, and place it before the cross of Jesus. (Take the time to pray about each aspect of grief you have been bearing, ensuring you specifically confess and release it before Him)

Father God, as we release this pain and sadness before You, please speak your Word to our hearts right now. (take a few moments to quietly listen for Him to speak to you)

Father, we receive right now by faith your comforting healing upon our hearts.

We look forward with anticipation to the great comfort to come at the Day of Jesus Return and in the future Jubilee.

In Jesus Name,

Amen

¹ *The Gates of Hell*, First Fruits of Zion, https://torahportions.ffoz.org/disciples/matthew/the-gates-of-hell.html (accessed Aug. 17, 2023)

² It is important to note that the Bible teaches two separate resurrections, "the Resurrection of Life" and the "Resurrection of Condemnation" (John 5:28-29). The second resurrection will take place 1'000 years after the first, and is described in Appendix 2 of this book.

Reflection Questions

1. What does it mean that the "gates of hell" will not prevail against the Church?
2. Why will the future Jubilee be a day of great joy?
3. In that great day of restoration, what will be the most special moment of restoration for you personally?

9

The Upside-Down Kingdom

A young girl in Tegucigalpa, Honduras, sits on her bed, playing her drum and singing a song to herself. Later that day, the little girl can hardly contain her excitement as she and her younger brother head to an exclusive music audition. Her dad dutifully returns a few hours later to collect them. To his horror, he discovers that the children are gone, kidnapped by child sex traffickers.

The box office hit movie *The Sound of Freedom,* is based on the true story of Tim Ballard and his efforts to save children such as these out of the hideous sex trade. There are today close to 30 million people caught as slaves within the rapidly booming global sex trade[1]. It is disturbing to consider the fact that there are more people in slavery today than at any other time in world history.

The film rightly encourages us to advocate for the victims of the sex trade, but anyone watching the film can feel overwhelmed by the vastness of the problem. While Tim Ballard was heroically able to save 120 kids from the trade, there remains millions trapped without hope.

At the end of the movie, we follow the little girl as she is finally reunited with her family and returned to her home. At home she finds a new toy drum and soon begins to sing her song again, the sound of freedom.

I believe there is coming a great Jubilee sound of freedom for the slaves and oppressed of this world. Not only will the slaves and captives be set free on that day, but the Jubilee will also sound judgment on the evildoers of this world, including those who have so wickedly oppressed these little ones.

In the words of Jesus:

> It would be better for them to be thrown into the sea with a millstone tied around their neck than to cause one of these little ones to stumble.
> (Luke 17:2, NIV)

The Day of Vengeance

> "The Spirit of the Lord God is upon Me....
> To proclaim the acceptable year of the Lord,
> And the day of vengeance of our God;"
> (Is 61:1-2)

The Messianic Judgement of our world is a key component of the promised Jubilee Redemption. To "*redeem*" in Hebrew doesn't just mean "*to buy back*" in terms of the Jubilee, but also to "*pay back*". In the Laws of Moses there is provision for a murderer to be killed by a relative of the victim. Our English Bibles call this relative "*the avenger of blood*", but in Hebrew it is literally "*the redeemer of blood*" (Num. 35:19). In other words, a redeemer would step forward to "settle the score" and undo the injustice done. And if there was no redeemer found, God himself would take up the cause of the oppressed and deal with the evildoers.

We find an example in the book of Jeremiah. In line with the commandments of the Jubilee, the wealthy announced that they would set their slaves free, but then later reneged on the deal. The slaves who had been jubilant at the initial announcement, would have been totally crushed by this turn of events. In return, God himself stepped up and judged these wicked oppressors, repaying them in kind by "releasing" them to the hands of their merciless enemies (Jer. 34:13-17).

The judgement of the wicked in Jeremiah's day is only a foretaste of the great judgement to come in that great future day. The Jubilee will therefore not only be the "year of the Lord's favour", but also the day of His vengeance.

The Judge is Coming

King David speaks of the great joy to come when the Lord finally comes as the Judge:

> Let the heavens rejoice, and let the earth be glad;... Let the field rejoice, and all that is in it.
> Then the trees of the woods shall rejoice before the Lord,
> For He is coming to judge the earth.
> (1 Chron 16:31-33)

While Christians tend to think of Jesus as "meek and mild", Messianic prophecies repeatedly portray Him as not only the coming King but also as the coming Judge of the world. Let us turn for example to the book of Isaiah:

> The Spirit of the Lord will rest on him—
> .....with righteousness he will judge the needy,
> with **justice he will give decisions for the poor of the earth.**
> He will strike the earth with the rod of his mouth;
> with **the breath of his lips he will slay the wicked.**
> (Is. 11:1-4, NIV emphasis added)

We see a similar theme repeated in the Psalms:

> The Lord has sworn And will not relent,
> "You are a priest forever
> According to the order of Melchizedek."
> The Lord is at Your right hand;
> **He shall execute kings** in the day of His wrath.
> He shall judge among the nations....
> **He shall execute the heads of many countries.**
> (Ps 110:4-6, emphasis added)

This era of judgment will be severe, but as evil is finally judged in this world, the result will be an amazing peace finally settling on this troubled planet:

> He shall judge between the nations,
> And rebuke many people;
> [then] they shall beat their swords into plowshares,
> And their spears into pruning hooks;
> Nation shall not lift up sword against nation,
> Neither shall they learn war anymore.
> (Is. 2:4)

The Upside-Down Kingdom

The Talmud tells a story of Joseph, the son of the sage Rabbi Yehoshua ben Levi, who became deathly ill and was thought to have died. When he finally regained consciousness, his father said to him: 'What did you see?' Joseph said: 'I saw a world turned upside down. What is above was below and what is below was above….' His father said to him: 'My son …you have seen the world clearly….'" [Talmud Bavli, Pesachim 50a]

The Jubilee speaks of the great day to come where this current world system will, as in the vision of the Rabbi's son, be turned upside down. The Psalmist speaks of the great hope of this day:

> Rest in the Lord, and wait patiently for Him;
> **Do not fret because of him who prospers** in his way,
> Because of the man who brings **wicked schemes to pass.**
> For **evildoers shall be cut off**;
> But those who **wait on the Lord,**
> They shall **inherit the earth.**
> For yet a little while and the **wicked shall be no more**;
> Indeed, you will look carefully for his place,
> But it shall be no more.
> But the meek shall inherit the earth,
> (Ps. 37:7-9, emphasis added)

We certainly must do what we can to resist and stop the global sex trade. Yet on the other hand the Psalmist exhorts us not to fret or be overwhelmed by this evil, reminding us of the hope that God will one day deal with these oppressors. Furthermore, the Psalmist assures us that while the wicked may rule for a while, they will one day be gone, and we will inherit this earth. While much of Christianity has had its expectation set on us leaving this planet with Heaven being our spiritual "promised land", instead the Psalmist speaks of the wicked being the ones removed, leaving us to rule this planet. That is certainly upside down to the expectation of many believers!

The New Testament Kingdom

We see this theme repeated in the New Testament writings. When Jesus finally sits enthroned in Jerusalem (Luke 1:32), the book of Revelation tells us that there will be a new chain of authority on this Earth:

> To him who overcomes I will grant to sit with Me on My throne
> (Rev. 3:21)
>
> And they lived and reigned with Christ for a thousand years
> (Rev. 20:4)

Jesus repeatedly told His followers that in the new world order, believers will be rewarded with varying positions of authority based on their faithfulness in this life:

> Then came the first, saying, 'Master, your mina has earned ten minas.' And he said to him, 'Well *done*, good servant; **because you were faithful** in a very little, have **authority over ten cities**.' And the second came, saying, 'Master, your mina has earned five minas.' Likewise he said to him, 'You also be over **five cities**.'
> (Luke 19:16-19, emphasis added)

If you are like me, the thought of physically ruling and reigning with Jesus in His future kingdom sounds both foreign and far-fetched. It is reasonable that *He* will reign, "*but who am I to rule with Him?*".

I have discovered a principle that may help us understand this future Kingdom in the context of our current day to day lives. The principle is that God always prepares us ahead of time for the tasks He has in store, even if we are not aware of this preparation at the time.

For example, when I started my studies at Bible College most of my fellow students were youth leaders. "*That will never be me*", I thought to myself. I was convinced that I lacked the dynamic personality needed for such a role. A few weeks into my course, our church's youth leader resigned unexpectedly from his position and within a few weeks I was appointed as the new leader.

As a youth leader, I discovered to my great surprise that I had the skills and abilities needed for the task. I came to realise that God had in fact been preparing me for a long time for this role. Years earlier, as a teenager, I had been a 'fly on the wall' observing the mechanics of how my youth pastor at the time was delegating responsibility, training up others, giving them opportunities and leading them as a group. Now all these ideas came flooding back to my mind and I realised that this was God's destiny for me and that I had been sovereignly prepared by Him for this task.

In the new upside-down world of Jesus' Kingdom, we will find that we too have been uniquely prepared for the tasks God has in mind. We will discover that the lessons we learnt in life, the character tests we faced, and the things we overcame (and even our mistakes too!) will all have prepared us for this very moment of ruling and reigning with Him.

The Great Rebuilding Project

In the lead up to the establishment of Jesus' Kingdom on Earth, cities and even entire nations will have been levelled to the ground and destroyed in the cataclysmic end time events (see for example Rev. 16:18-20).

During His reign, I believe Jesus will enact one of the greatest rebuilding projects the world has ever known. Not only will he rebuild and restore the land of Israel, but also the nations of the earth will be restored[2].

According to Isaiah's Jubilee prophecy:

> And they shall rebuild the old ruins,
> They shall raise up the former desolations,
> And they shall repair the ruined cities,
> The desolations of many generations.
> (Is. 61:4)

In the coming Kingdom the Master will need engineers, builders, gardeners, architects, cooks, teachers, planners and countless other trades and talents to make this massive reconstruction effort succeed. While traditional gnostic influenced Christianity may leave us feeling guilty about "non-spiritual" tasks that we enjoy doing (such as cooking, gardening and tinkering with our tools), the Jubilee perspective reveals that these are in fact God-given skills which will be used to serve the King in His coming kingdom.

As Theologian Tom Wright eloquently explains:

> Forget those images about lounging around playing harps. There will be work to do and we shall relish doing it. All the skills and talents which we have put to God's service in this present life - and perhaps, too, the interests and likings we gave up because they conflicted with our vocation - will be enhanced and ennobled and given back to us to be exercised for His glory.[3]

An Era of Peace and Restoration

We have seen that after much suffering, our planet will be restored and rejuvenated and become the beautiful place God intended from the beginning.

In that Day, Jesus will sit on the throne of Israel bringing a new world order of peace:

> But the meek shall **inherit the earth**,
> And shall delight themselves in the **abundance of peace**.
> (Ps. 37:11, emphasis added)

The "abundant peace" of the Kingdom does not just imply the absence of war. The Hebrew word "shalom" also means to make good, fully restore and make restitution[4]. In other words, the Age to come will be a time of complete, full restitution and restoration of our broken world.

In that day, God will comfort the broken-hearted and finally put an end to the evils of this world such as the global sex trade. And in that beautiful Age of Restoration, Jesus will rule from Jerusalem with His faithful Saints ruling by His side.

Is it any wonder that Jesus taught us to pray regularly for the coming of this Kingdom?

> **Your kingdom** come.
> Your will be done
> **On earth** as it is in heaven.
> (Matt 6:10, emphasis added)

May that day come soon - Amen!

God's Heart of Restoration

I believe God has a huge heart for restoration. Whereas the enemy has been hellbent on destroying people, families, cities and nations, God is at work to restore all things to Himself (as long as people are willing).

In our next chapter we are going to discover that not only is the Restoration of Israel at the core of the Jubilee, it also dramatically impacts our understanding of key New Testament prophecies.

[1] Richardson, Joel, *When a Jew Rules the World*, p. 79

[2] Notably, the wicked city of Babylon will not be rebuilt. See Is. 13:20

[3] Wright, Tom. *Surprised By Hope*, p. 173

[4] Hershey, Doug. *The True Meaning of Shalom*, Jan. 3rd, 2020. Fellowship of Israel Related Ministries, https://firmisrael.org/learn/the-meaning-of-shalom/ (accessed Aug. 19th, 2023).

Reflection Questions

1. In what way is the Jubilee linked to the coming judgment of this world?
2. Describe in your own words what will happen to the wicked and to the righteous in the coming judgment?
3. What practical skills has God given you which you may be able to use in His coming Kingdom here on earth?

10

Regathering The Exiles

As the Nazi death camps were being liberated at the end of World War II, a BBC radio crew encountered a group of holocaust survivors staggering their way out of a death camp. Realising they were being recorded, these emaciated survivors summoned the last ounces of strength in their bodies to sing the song *HaTikvah*[1]. Listen to its poignant refrain:

> "Our hope is not yet lost,
> The hope of two thousand years,
> To be a free nation in our land,
> The land of Zion and Jerusalem."

These holocaust survivors wanted the world to know the hope that was still beating in their heart. Their hope was that they would, after so many dark years of exile, finally return home to their God-given land of Zion and Jerusalem. The *HaTikvah*, originally written in the late 1800's, later became Israel's national anthem.

In this chapter we will discover how this deep yearning of the Jewish nation is rooted in the promises of the Bible, is central to the Jubilee, and is a matter that remains very close to God's heart.

You will find no rest.....

> Then the Lord will scatter you among all peoples, from one end of the earth to the other... And among those nations you shall find no rest, nor shall the sole of your foot have a resting place; but there the Lord will give you a trembling heart, failing eyes, and anguish of soul.
> (Deut. 28:64-65)

In the aftermath of the Roman destruction of Jerusalem, the Jews were forcibly sent into world-wide exile. As Moses predicted, this exile was anything but peaceful.

Across Europe, Jews learned to dread the annual Easter "Passion" plays, in which Churches re-enacted Jesus' death at the hands of the "wicked" Jews. Afterwards parishioners would descend on the Jewish quarters of their towns and villages to enact revenge on the "Christ-killers" in riots that became known as pogroms.

Jews became the scapegoats of society and were blamed for all manner of evil. They were accused of kidnapping and murdering Gentile children to use their blood in the making of unleavened bread[2]. They were portrayed as evil unscrupulous money lenders, such as the hideous Shylock in Shakespeare's play "The Merchant of Venice", who demanded a "pound of flesh" as interest payment[3]. Jews were blamed for the black death plague, which claimed between 25-50 million victims across Europe[4]. These were but a few of many malicious rumours that blended with Christian anti-Semitic theology to produce a toxic combination. As soldiers from Christian Europe conquered Jerusalem during the Crusades, they infamously gathered the local Jews and forced them into a synagogue building. The Crusaders proceeded to light fire to the building, watching it burn to the ground with the Jews inside, all the while singing the hymn "Christ, we adore Thee"[5]. Next came the horrific torture of Jews during Spain's 350 year Inquisition[6,] and ultimately the murder of 6 million Jews by "Christian" Germany during the Holocaust. One Holocaust survivor relates how two German soldiers in his concentration camp would single him out for a beating every single day, except on Sundays when they went to church. He vividly remembers the crucifix he saw dangling around the neck of one of the soldiers, and years later told his son, "*I will never believe in Jesus*". Given this history of antisemitism, it is no wonder that many Jews to this day harbour a deep suspicion towards Christianity.

Throughout their exile, Jewish communities regularly faced forced expulsions from towns, cities and even nations of Europe. For example, England expelled her Jews in 1290 for almost 400 years, France expelled her Jews in 1306 and 1394 lasting until 1789. Spain and Portugal expelled over 100'000 Jews in 1492-1497, and Jews were banned from living in Russia from the 15th Century until 1772[7].

It is truly nothing less than a miracle that the Jewish people have survived the above catalogue of violence and atrocities. King Frederick the Great of Prussia once asked his pastor for one single irrefutable proof of God. The pastor answered with two simple words "The Jews"[8]. The Pastor must have been familiar with God's promise to Jeremiah that as long as the sun and moon are in the sky, the Jews will remain a people before Him (Jer. 31:36-37). And against all odds, and despite horrendous persecution, the Jewish people have survived as testament to the faithfulness of God's Word.

The Hope of the Regathering

Down through the ages the suffering exiles of Israel have been able to draw hope from over sixty passages of the Old Testament promising their return.

These prophecies paint a dramatic picture of the extent of their regathering:

- It will be a miraculous return more dramatic than the original Exodus from Egypt.
  "It shall no more be said, 'The Lord lives who brought up the children of Israel from the land of Egypt,' but, 'The Lord lives who brought up the children of Israel from the land of the north and from all the lands where He had driven them"
  (Jer. 16:14-16)
- The Regathering will be on a global scale.
  "I will bring your descendants from the east, And gather you from the west; I will say to the north, 'Give them up!' And to the south, 'Do not keep them back!' Bring My sons from afar, And My daughters from the ends of the earth."
  (Is. 43:5-6)
- The Messiah Himself, with the help of the Gentiles, will bring His people back to their land.
  "[The Messiah] will assemble the outcasts of Israel,
  And gather together the dispersed of Judah
  From the four corners of the earth."
  (Is. 11:12)
  "Behold, I will lift My hand in an oath to the nations...
  They shall bring your sons in their arms,
  And your daughters shall be carried on their shoulders [9]
  (Is. 49:22-23)
- God will gain great glory in the sight of all nations because of this miracle.
  "the nations shall know that I am the Lord," says the Lord God....
  "when..... I will take you from among the nations, gather you out of all countries, and bring you into your own land."
  (Ezek. 36:21-23)

Some say the Regathering of the Jews from Babylon under Ezra and Nehemiah is the fulfilment of these prophecies, but it should be noted that this regathering was far from global in scope and nor does it meet the other prophetic criteria.

Others point to Israel's miraculous return in our modern times as a fulfilment of these prophecies. And while Israel's modern-day regathering certainly is prophetic and attests to God's faithfulness to His people Israel, it too falls short of the full picture portrayed by Biblical prophecy.

The Regathering and the Messianic Age

Isaiah puts the promised Regathering of Israel firmly in the context of the Messianic era. Isaiah describes the peaceful nature of the Messianic reign with nations laying down their weapons, the lion lying *'down with the lamb'* (Is. 11:6-9) and Israel being regathered:

> It shall come to pass in that day
> That the Lord shall set His hand again the second time
> To **recover the remnant of His people who are left**,
> From Assyria and Egypt... and the islands of the sea.
> He will set up a banner for the nations,
> And **will assemble the outcasts of Israel,**
> And **gather together** the dispersed of Judah
> From the **four corners of the earth.**
> (Is. 11:11-12, emphasis added)

In addition, many prophecies intertwine Israel's regathering with her spiritual restoration, something which obviously has not happened yet on a national scale.

For example, Ezekiel predicts:

> For I will take you from among the nations, gather you out of all countries, and **bring you into your own land.** Then I will sprinkle clean water on you, and you shall be clean; I will cleanse you from all your filthiness and from all your idols. **I will give you a new heart** and put a new spirit within you; I will take the heart of stone out of your flesh and give you a heart of flesh. I will put My Spirit within you and cause you to walk in My statutes, and you will keep My judgments and do them. Then you shall dwell in the land that I gave to your fathers; **you shall be My people, and I will be your God.**
> (Ezek. 36:24-28, emphasis added)

The Bible is clear that it is only at the end of time, that Israel will be saved as a nation (see Zec. 12:10 and Rom. 11:26). In other words, Israel will be both saved as a nation and regathered to their land at Jesus' return.

The Regathering of the Jewish people to their ancient homeland is not simply a nationalistic dream. Rather it is a central theme of Old Testament prophecy yet to be fulfilled, and its scale and associated events place it firmly in the context of Jesus' return.

The Regathering and the Jubilee

The Return of the Jewish people to their ancient inheritance is also at the very heart of the Jubilee message. It is therefore no surprise that we find the theme of redemption appear throughout the prophecies of this great return. See for example these words of Isaiah:

> But now, thus says the Lord, who created you, O Jacob,
> And He who formed you, O Israel:
> "Fear not, for I have **redeemed** you...
> ....**I will bring your descendants** from the east,
> And gather you from the west;
> I will say to the north, 'Give them up!'
> And to the south, 'Do not keep them back!'
> Bring My sons from afar,
> And My daughters from the ends of the earth
> (Is 43:1,5-6, emphasis added)

Furthermore, Isaiah declares that this end time regathering will be at the sound of the trumpet:

> And it shall come to pass in that day....
> you will be gathered one by one,
> O you children of Israel.
> So it shall be in that day:
> The **great trumpet** will be blown;
> They will come, who are about to perish in the land of Assyria,
> And they who are outcasts in the land of Egypt,
> And shall worship the Lord in the holy mount at Jerusalem.
> (Is 27:12-13, emphasis added)

The Jubilee in ancient Israel was always announced with a special sounding of the trumpet, marking the return of the Jewish people to the land of their inheritance. Isaiah is clear that the final regathering of the Jews will likewise be linked to the trumpet sound of the Jubilee.

Interestingly, Orthodox Jews to this day pray three times a day for this event, specifically linking it to shofar (trumpet) sound:

> "Sound the **great shofar for our freedom**, raise the banner to gather our exiles and gather us together from the four corners of the earth. Blessed are You, Our Lord, Who gathers in the dispersed of His people Israel."
> [10th Benediction of the Shemoneh Esrei, emphasis added][10]

Entering the Promised Land

The Hebrew word yobel (jubilee) only occurs in five distinct passages in the Bible. Three of these passages are technical descriptions of the laws surrounding the jubilee. We previously studied the fourth mention which we found in the story of God descending physically on Mount Sinai. The final mention of the Hebrew word yobel is found in the most defining moment of Joshua's life and leadership.

After Moses' death, Joshua had the daunting challenge of leading the people of Israel to inherit the promised land. Ahead of them lay a seemingly insurmountable obstacle, the formidable city of Jericho. Preparing for battle, Joshua encounters the Angel of the Lord, who gives him very specific and highly unusual battle instructions.

Before we look at these instructions, let us briefly recap some Jubilee basics. The Jubilee was to take place in the context of a calendar where God instructed His people to farm the land for six years and then rest the land in the seventh year. After the completion of seven such seven-year cycles, in the 50th year the Jubilee would be proclaimed.

God's rather unusual battle instructions at Jericho were for the Israelites to march around the city for seven days and then finally seven times on the seventh day. Do you see a pattern emerging?

Furthermore, the Lord instructed:

> It shall come to pass, when they make a **long blast with the ram's horn**, and when you hear the sound of the trumpet, that all the people shall shout with a great shout; then the wall of the city will fall down flat. And the people shall go up every man straight before him.
> (Josh 6:5, emphasis added)

Throughout this chapter of Joshua, the Hebrew word *yobel* (jubilee) is used again and again in place of the word for trumpet. This clearly shows that the walls of Jericho collapsed not at the sound of just any trumpet, but specifically at the majestic sounding of the Jubilee trumpet. And as this trumpet sounded and the walls came tumbling down, Israel could finally march right into their inheritance. It truly was a Jubilee for the redeemed people of Israel!

Jesus and Joshua

Is there a prophetic application to the story of the Battle of Jericho? Is there a prophetic significance to this final direct mention of the word jubilee in the Bible?

Like the walls of Jericho resisted the ancient Israelites, so Israel's modern day regathering has been strongly opposed by both the Islamic world and much of the Western world. But in that great day when the trumpet sounds, enemy opposition to Israel's regathering will come tumbling down like those ancient walls of Jericho.

In Hebrew the name Jesus is simply another form of the name Joshua. And it will be through this greater Joshua, this great redeemer of God's people, that Israel will finally enter its full inheritance. Then those long years of exile and persecution will finally be over, and then the hope of Israel will find its fulfilment as they take possession of the promised land with their Messiah at the helm.

With All God's Heart

The prophet Jeremiah gives us a unique glimpse of how God feels about the restoration of Israel to her land:

> Behold, I will gather them out of all countries where I have driven them in My anger, in My fury, and in great wrath; I will bring them back to this place, and I will cause them to dwell safely. They shall be My people, and I will be their God..... And I will make an everlasting covenant with them.... and I will **assuredly plant them in this land, with all My heart and with all My soul.**'
> (Jer. 32:37-40, emphasis added)

Israel's return to her ancient land is the only thing throughout all of Scripture that God says He will do with all His heart and all His soul. In other words, God is passionate about His land and He strongly desires to restore His people to it. While some Christian theologies teach that God is finished with the Jews because of their sins and many failures, the Bible gives testament to the fact that God has not rejected His people (Rom. 11:1). Instead, He is at work to restore them to Himself and to their destiny in the land He has for them.

The disciples once asked Jesus to teach them how to pray.

Jesus' answer is today known as the Lord's Prayer:

> Our Father in heaven,
> Hallowed be Your name.
> Your kingdom come.
> Your will be done
> On earth as it is in heaven.
> Give us this day our daily bread...
> (Matt. 6:9-11)

Next time you pray the Lord's Prayer, bear in mind that His will and passionate desire is for the complete restoration of Israel to her land and to Himself. In other words, if we are to pray according to God's heart and according to the model of Jesus' prayer, then we should allow the Lord to make the regathering a central part of our prayers. We should weep for Israel's current exile and suffering, entreat the Lord for mercy upon her and rejoice in the promises of her future restoration.

May that day come soon!

The Regathering in the New Testament

In this chapter we have seen how the final regathering of the Jewish people will occur at Jesus' return as the Jubilee trumpet sounds its great blast.

This theme of the regathering is prominent in Old Testament prophecy, but in our next chapter we are going to make a revolutionary discovery as to where it fits in the New Testament's depiction of the end of days.

¹ Recording available at *BERGEN BELSEN HATIKVAH*, The Israel Forever Foundation. https://israelforever.org/gallery/music/bergen_belsen_hatikvah/ (accessed Sep. 4th, 2023)

² See *Blood Libel*, Wikepedia, https://en.wikipedia.org/wiki/Blood_libel (accessed Sep. 12, 2024)

³ See *The Merchant of Venice*, Wikipedia, https://en.wikipedia.org/wiki/The_Merchant_of_Venice (accessed Sep. 12, 2024)

⁴ *Medieval antisemitism*, The Holocaust Explained, https://www.theholocaustexplained.org/anti-semitism/medieval-antisemitism/the-black-death/, (accessed Sep. 12, 2024)

⁵ Keasler, Keas. *Father, Forgive Us (part 1)*, http://www.keaskeasler.com/2010/04/father-forgive-us-part-1/ (accessed Sep. 24, 2024)

⁶ *Spanish Inquisition Key Facts*, Britannica, https://www.britannica.com/summary/Spanish-Inquisition-Key-Facts (accessed Sep. 12, 2024)

⁷ See Haim Hillel Ben-Sasson, *Expulsions of Jews*, Jewish Virtual Library, https://www.jewishvirtuallibrary.org/expulsions (accessed Aug, 1, 2023)

⁸ *Essay: Jun. 25, 1965*, Time, https://time.com/archive/6627599/essay-jun-25-1965/ (accessed Sep. 12, 2024)

⁹ A friend of mine served as a volunteer in Russia assisting Jews returning to Israel. Once, at a Moscow train station, she was assisting an elderly Jewish grandmother off a train, and literally picked her up on her shoulders to carry her down the steep steps. As she was carrying this elderly Jew, she was deeply touched to recall this specific prophecy of Gentiles carrying Jews on their shoulders.

¹⁰ Quoted from Travis, Daniel. *Visions of Jerusalem: Understanding the Middle Blessings of Shemoneh Esrei II*
The Tenth Blessing: Return. May 6, 2019 . https://torah.org/learning/tefilah-tenthblessing/ (accessed Sep. 16. 2023)

Reflection Questions

1. In the Jewish world, the sad history of Christian anti-semitism is vividly remembered. How can Christians best make amends to the Jewish people and rebuild a relationship with them?
2. Name five key features of the prophesied regathering of the Jewish people.
3. Why is the regathering of Israel so central to God's heart?

11

The Gathering of the Saints

My wife and I were living in Melbourne with our baby twins at the outbreak of the Covid-19 pandemic. Little did we know that our city was about to endure six severe lockdowns. Between March 2020 and October 2021, Melbourne became the world's most locked down city spending an unenviable 262 days in lockdown.

During these lockdowns I started attending an online Bible study group called the Torah Portion. One morning our Bible study leader, Ps. Greg Cumming, asked an unforgettable question: *"The regathering of Israel is a central theme of Old Testament prophecy. Where then do we find this theme referenced in the New Testament? Did the New Testament writers forget to reference this major theme?"*

As we continued the Bible study, we attempted to put ourselves in the shoes of Jesus' first century listeners, hearing His Words of prophecy for the first time. Bearing in mind the centrality of the regathering of the Jewish people in the prophetic texts, we considered afresh these words of Jesus on the Mount of Olives:

> Immediately after the tribulation of those days .... the sign of the Son of Man will appear in heaven, and then all the **tribes of the earth will mourn**, and they will see the Son of Man coming on the clouds of heaven with power and great glory. And He will send His angels with a **great sound of a trumpet**, and **they will gather together His elect from the four winds**, from one end of heaven to the other.
> (Matt 24:29-31, emphasis added)

During that Bible study, I began to realise that Jesus' Jewish listeners would have immediately drawn connections from His Words to what was already clearly and repeatedly predicted by the prophets - namely that God would one day gather the scattered Jews back to their ancient homeland at the end of times.

Jesus' reference to the "*tribes of the earth*" mourning at His return further strengthens the links to this prophesied regathering. While this phrase is rather ambiguous in English and could refer to Gentiles or Jews, in Hebrew, the phrase would have been the tribes of the "*aretz*" which exclusively refers to the tribes of Israel[1]. In other words, Jesus is in this passage speaking of the Jewish people as firstly being the ones who will be mourning in repentance as they see Him coming (see Zec. 12:10), and secondly as being the elect who the Messiah regathers at the sound of the trumpet.

But what about Gentile believers? We will come to that soon, but first, let's turn to a key prophecy of Jeremiah for further insight into this end time regathering.

What could be Greater than the Exodus?

> "Therefore behold, the days are coming," says the Lord, "that it shall no more be said, 'The Lord lives who brought up the children of Israel from the land of Egypt,' but, 'The Lord lives who brought up the children of Israel from the land of the north and from all the lands where He had driven them.'
> (Jer 16:14-16)

To date the modern regathering of Israel is the closest we have ever come to a fulfilment of Jeremiah's prophecy. Since 1948, over three million Jews have returned to their ancient homeland from all over the world. This long-awaited restoration has seen its share of miracles and Christians have played a central role in helping to facilitate the return[2]. However, the miracles of the Exodus are still rightly remembered and celebrated above and beyond the modern-day regathering of Israel.

What would it take for this future regathering to be more miraculous than the Exodus from Egypt? Putting aside for a moment your own personal view of the Rapture[3], imagine for a moment the following scenario. After a time of great evil upon the earth, Jesus appears in the sky on His way to set up His Kingdom on Earth. All over the world people look up at the sight of Jesus in the clouds with myriads of majestic angels surrounding Him. Suddenly, a thunderous worldwide trumpet blast is heard. At its sound, Jews from all over the world are literally picked up and brought through the air towards their promised land in Israel. On their way, they meet the radiant Jesus in the sky and turn to Him in repentance before landing in Jerusalem together with the coming King.

This scenario may seem foreign to us, but it certainly would fulfil Jeremiah's criteria of an end time regathering far more spectacular than the original Exodus from Egypt.

What then about Gentile believers? Where do we fit in this picture?

The Gathering of the Saints

Let's briefly analyse some familiar words from Paul the Apostle:

> For the Lord Himself will descend from heaven with a shout, with the voice of an archangel, and with the trumpet of God. And the **dead in Christ will rise first**. Then **we** who are alive and remain **shall be caught up together** with them in the clouds to meet the Lord in the air. And thus we shall always be with the Lord. Therefore comfort one another with these words.
> (1 Thes. 4:16-18, emphasis added)

As the trumpet of Jesus' Return sounds, the first thing that happens is that the "*dead will rise*". In other words, their spirits will be united with their bodies again as they appear with the Lord in the air.

Paul goes on to explain to his audience of Gentile and Jewish believers in Jesus that **we** who are alive "*will meet them in the air*" and will "*always be with the Lord*". In other words, Gentile believers will definitely be part of this worldwide ingathering.

Isaiah the prophet concurs. Isaiah 56, a chapter dedicated to Gentile God-fearers and God's acceptance of them, explains that God will "*bring*" these Gentiles to His holy mountain for "*My house shall be called a house of prayer for all nations.*" (v. 7). In the very next breath, Isaiah links the ingathering of the Gentiles with the ingathering of Israel:

> The Lord God, who gathers the outcasts of Israel, says, "Yet I will gather to him others besides those who are gathered to him.
> (Is. 56:8)

Where are We Going?

Continuing our scenario, let's visualise the scene as millions of believers and Jews ascend into the sky at the sound of the trumpet. A question that is bound to be on everyone's lips is "*where are we going*"?

Paul says that we will "*meet the Lord in the air*", and from then on always be with Him. Many in the Church have understood these verses to mean that we will from now on be in Heaven, however a closer understanding of the phrase "*meet them in the air*" reveals a different understanding. The word translated to "meet" in this passage is used to describe the custom of delegations leaving a city to meet a guest of great importance who is on his way to town. The delegation would greet the honoured person before accompanying them back to town. Using the very same Greek word, the Bible tells the story of Paul's journey to Rome, and how a delegation from the city came out to meet him and accompany him back (Acts 28:14-16). At His return, Jesus will be the person of great honour who is coming, and it seems that the Church and Israel will together make up the delegation coming to meet and greet Him before His feet even touch the ground.

When Paul says we will from then on "*always be with the Lord*", it is important to remember where Jesus is going. He is coming to Earth to establish His Kingdom, to fulfil the promises and prophecies of Scripture and to sit on the throne of His father David. And we - according to Paul - will be coming with Him to His great coronation event in Jerusalem!

The Wedding Supper of the Lamb

A recurring theme of Jesus' end time teachings is the coming wedding supper of the Lamb (see for example Matt. 9:15, 22:2-12, Luke 12:36). According to Jesus, this special meal will feature both Jews and Gentiles in attendance:

> I say to you that many will come from the east and the west, and will take their places at the feast with Abraham, Isaac and Jacob in the kingdom of heaven.
> (Matt. 8:11, NIV)

We discussed in chapter 6 how the phrase "the Kingdom of Heaven" is in its Jewish context referring to God's kingdom coming to earth. And in the Words of Jesus, as God's kingdom is established in Jerusalem, the wedding feast will also take place here, bringing together Jewish and Gentile followers of the Messiah. The prophet Isaiah concurs:

> And in **this mountain** the Lord of hosts will make **for all people a feast** of choice pieces, a feast of wines on the lees, of fat things full of marrow, of well-refined wines on the lees. And He will destroy ... the veil that is spread over all nations. He will **swallow up death forever**...
> (Isaiah 25:6-8, emphasis added)

Isaiah makes it clear that this choice feast happens in the context of the Resurrection of the Dead, and the venue will be none other than God's Holy Hill in Jerusalem. And those invited will not only be Israel, but also Gentile believers from every nation sitting and eating with the patriarchs of Israel.

For further insight, we turn to author and end time teacher Joel Richardson, who compares this future event to the pattern set at Mount Sinai during the days of Moses. At Sinai, God's glory physically descended on the mountain top. The elders of Israel proceeded to ascend the mountain where they "*saw God, and they ate and drank*" (Ex. 24:11). Joel points out that this meal was for a purpose, it was a covenant meal, sealing the events of Sinai as a wedding between Israel and her God[4]. The prophets of Israel later looked back to this event as their basis for accusing unfaithful Israel of "adultery" as she was breaking her marriage covenant with God.

The coming wedding banquet here on Earth will be for the same purpose, namely that it will mark the renewal of God's Marriage Covenant with Israel. This covenant, known as the New Covenant, is extended to include believers from all nations (see Jer. 31:31-34). This explains why we find Gentiles attending this special feast alongside the patriarchs and the faithful of Israel.

Keeping the Context in Mind

The understanding of the Jubilee, the Resurrection of the Dead, the wedding banquet and God's Kingdom being established here on Earth all come together to bring a very different context of the Rapture than what is commonly taught in churches today.

Divorced from its Jewish context, the classic Rapture scripture verses seem to indicate a gathering of the Church separated from unbelieving Israel. But the more I study the larger context of the Resurrection of the Dead and the Ingathering of Israel at the Messiah's Return, the more I am convinced that all these events are one and the same, all finding their fulfilment in the great sounding of the Jubilee Trumpet. However, I would encourage you as the reader to form your own conclusions as you study these words of Prophecy.

Are We There yet?

So far in this book we have examined the Jubilee expectation at the first coming of Jesus, as well as the perspective it provides of His return.

In our next chapter we are going to dive into the prophetic restoration of Israel which has already been taking place, and discover how it lines up with the Jubilee time frame.

Has the Jubilee already begun? Find out in the next chapter!

[1] Richardson, Joel. *Sinai to Zion: The Untold Story of the Triumphant Return of Jesus,* p. 331

[2] For inspiring stories about the miraculous Christian involvement in this return, see "*Operation Exodus*" by Gustav Scheller.

[3] In essence, the doctrine of the Rapture teaches that Jesus will suddenly come and take His people (the Church) back to Heaven with Him. Those who remain on the Earth, will then go through the Great Tribulation. At the end of the Tribulation, Jesus will return, judge evil and setup His throne on Earth.

I am personally saddened by the great divisions and in-fighting within the church over the topic of the Rapture and End Time events. As a result, many main stream churches today shy away from the topic all together.

As you consider the material in this book, I would encourage you to put aside your understanding of the Rapture for a moment to consider how the teachings of Jesus and the Apostles would have been understood by the early Church in the context of Old Testament prophecy and the Coming Jubilee.

[4] Joel Richardson writes extensively about the wedding feast in his excellent book '*Sinai to Zion, The Untold Story of the Triumphant Return of Jesus*', see especially chapter 17. This book is available via Amazon and Christian retailers, as well being a free download at www.joelstrumpet.com

Reflection Questions

1. What would it look like for Israel's regathering to become greater than the original exodus from Egypt?
2. Do you agree that the Rapture passages of the New Testament would have been understood by their original Jewish listeners as referring to the established prophecies of the final Regathering of Israel? Give reasons why or why not.

12

The Restoration Has Begun

"Repent therefore... that He may send Jesus Christ... whom heaven must receive until the times of restoration of all things"
Acts 3:19-21

As Peter spoke these words of the promised restoration of Israel, neither he nor his listeners could have known what was in store for the Jewish people. Over the following decades, a series of rebellions sparked devastating wars between the Jews and the mighty Roman empire, culminating in the final Jewish rebellion being squashed in AD 135. Roman Historian Cassius Dio records the carnage and the mass devastation inflicted on the land of Israel:

> 580,000 men were slain in the various raids and battles, and the number of those that perished by famine, disease and fire was past finding out, Thus nearly the whole of Judaea was made desolate.
> (Cassius Dio, History of Rome, 69.14.1-2)[1]

It was utter tragedy for Israel as the Jews lost their God-given land, lost God's Holy Temple and the use of the language of Hebrew. The surviving Jews were scattered throughout the nations, where they faced repeated vicious cycles of persecution. During this time, the Church taught God had finished with the Jews, and that their present suffering and exile was proof of the divine rejection. Martin Luther for example described the Jews as "accursed and miserable"[2]. Instead of the Jews, it was taught, God has now chosen the Church. Such Replacement Theology sees all the glorious Old Testament Prophecies concerning Israel as no longer applying to her, but rather applying to either the Church or to Jesus. This teaching left believers with no expectation of a restoration of Israel ever occuring.

The late 1800's must have been shocking for many Christians as they unexpectedly began to hear reports of God restoring the Jews to their land, their national identity and their language. And as the restoration of Israel gathered pace after the birth of the nation in 1948, the strongholds of Replacement Theology began to crumble. Rays of light began to shine through as Bible believers realised the age-old truth of the Apostle Paul's words:

> I ask then: Did God reject his people? By no means!
> (Rom 11:1, NIV)

In this chapter we are going to study some of the highlights of Israel's modern day restoration. We will also discover how this restoration followed closely the Jubilee timeframe and was also linked to a similar move of God within the Church.

What is the meaning of this unprecedented restoration of Israel and the Church, and how does it relate to the Jubilee and the Return of Jesus?

The Restoration Begins

In the year 1897, the first Zionist World Congress was held in Basel, Switzerland, uniting together Jewish leadership to actively seek the establishment of a national home in Palestine. So significant was this event, that its leader Theodor Herzl wrote in his diary:

> "At Basel, I founded the Jewish State. If I said this aloud today, I would be greeted by universal laughter. In five years, perhaps, and certainly in fifty years, everyone will perceive it."[3]
> Theodor Herzl, Diary entry, Sep. 1, 1897

Exactly 50 years later, as Herzl had predicted, the UN voted to partition Palestine into a Jewish and an Arab state, leading to the birth of Israel in the following year of 1948. Is it a co-incidence that this restoration was taking place within a Jubilee time frame of 50 years?

Key events surrounding Israel's conquest of her land followed the same pattern. In 1917, British and Anzac forces were fighting the Turks in Beersheba and thanks to a daring charge by the Anzac light horse brigade experienced a miraculous breakthrough. This became the tipping point from which the entire land was liberated from 400 years of Ottoman Turkish rule. In the UK on that very same day, Oct. 31, 1917, the British war cabinet met and decided to give the Jews a homeland in Palestine[4]. Two days later Lord Arthur Balfour penned his famous Balfour declaration, declaring that Britain *'view with favour the establishment in Palestine of a national home for the Jewish people'*[5] laying the foundation for international recognition of the Jewish national right to a homeland in Palestine[6].

50 years later the Jubilee pattern continued through another significant military miracle. Israel was at this point a tiny nation, vulnerable to Arab attacks from the mountains of Judea which were under Jordanian control[7]. The surrounding Arab nations were join-

ing forces together under Egyptian President Nasser's command and were proudly declaring their ambition to destroy the Jewish state once and for all.

In the looming conflict, the odds were stacked against Israel, as the Arab armies boasted twice as many men, five times as many tanks (5,000 vs 1,000), and four times more aircraft (900 vs 196). Straining under the tension, Israel's Army Chief of Staff, Yitzhak Rabin, suffered a nervous breakdown. Attempting to calm the nerves of the nation, Israeli Prime Minister Levi Eschol addressed the nation. But his bumbling, stuttering speech did little to instill confidence in the Israel public, quite the opposite. During those dark days, public parks in Jerusalem were designated for mass graves, in anticipation of casualties exceeding 20,000 men.

Few could predict the miraculous turn around which was about to take place. Bestselling author Joel Rosenberg summarises what happened next as war broke out on June 5th, 1967:

> "In six days, the Jewish people defended themselves, destroyed their enemies, tripled their land; recaptured control of Jerusalem for the first time in 2,000 years and on the seventh day they rested'[8]

It was a miracle of Biblical proportions! Not only did it follow the 50-year Jubilee pattern, but it also lead to the restoration of much of Israel's ancient homeland including Judea and Samaria as well as most important of all, the old city of Jerusalem.

As battle hardened Jewish soldiers entered Jerusalem, they found themselves suddenly overwhelmed by the moment. Coming face to face with the Western Wall of the Temple Mount, tears began to stream down the faces of even the hardest atheists among them. Jews who had never uttered a prayer in their lives were swept up in the moment, asking their comrades to lead them in their very first prayers.

Fittingly, the head of Israel's army chaplains, Rabbi Shlomo Goren, pulled out his shofar and sounded it from the Western Wall. Rabbi Goren excitedly addressed the troops:

> This is the day we have hoped for, let us rejoice and be glad in His salvation. The vision of all generations is being realized before our eyes: The city of God, the site of the Temple, the Temple Mount and the Western Wall, the symbol of the nation's **redemption**, have been **redeemed** today by you, heroes of the Israel Defense Forces. ... In the name of the entire Jewish people in Israel and the Diaspora, I hereby recite with supreme joy, Blessed art Thou, O Lord our God, King of the universe, who has kept us alive, who has preserved us, and enabled us to reach this day. This year in Jerusalem – rebuilt![9]

Rabbi Goren then proceeded up to the Temple Mount where he approached IDF commander Uzi Narkiss. "*In preparation for the imminent Messianic era*", he stated, "*the IDF should utilize its explosives on hand to demolish the mosques on the Temple Mount*"[10]. In a stunning turn of events, Rabbi Goren's request was flatly rejected and control of the Temple Mount handed swiftly back to the Muslims.

Nevertheless the 1967 war saw Israel gain and retain control of Judea, Samaria and Jerusalem, and this restoration of Israel's heart land followed the Jubilee pattern of restoration, exactly 50 years after the Beersheba victory of 1917.

Continuing the Jubilee restoration pattern, US President Donald J. Trump, announced recognition of Jerusalem as Israel's capital in 2017, moving the US embassy to Jerusalem. At the time of writing, three other nations have followed the U.S. lead recognising Jerusalem as Israel's inheritance, and more nations are expected to follow[11].

The Church in the Dark Ages

We are living in a time when God is not only restoring Israel, but also the Church. This restoration carries strong ties to Israel's restoration and also has its own links to the Jubilee cycles.

During the dark ages, the Church lost much of its "inheritance", as the Bible became inaccessible to all but the elite and as strange teachings emanated from the pulpits. The Gifts of the Spirit were seen as dead, and miracles and healings were rare.

A critical turning point happened on the 31st of October 1517, when Martin Luther nailed his 95 theses to the Church door in Wittenburg, protesting the wayward teachings of the Catholic Church. This event was so pivotal in the launch of the Protestant reformation that it has come to be commemorated every year on the 31st of October as Reformation Day.

The Protestant movement helped restore the Bible into the hands of the common people and over the succeeding centuries began to restore much biblical truth that had been lost. Understanding of Bible prophecy began to grow within the Church. As a result, Christian supporters of the Restoration of Israel were present at the pivotal World Zionist Congress in 1897.

As the British and Anzac forces conquered Beersheba on the 31st of October 1917, it was Christian Zionists within the British government who on the very same day brought about the government decision behind the Balfour declaration. All this happened on the very day of the 400th anniversary of the Reformation, or in other words, the eighth Jubilee of Luther's reformation movement. It is certainly no co-incidence that the Reformation of the Church and the Restoration of Israel are linked in this way.

The Parallel Restoration

As the Hebrew language was being restored, the language of the Spirit - known as speaking in tongues - was restored to the Church. As Israel began to experience miracle after miracle on the battlefield, the Church was touched by an amazing healing revival. As Jerusalem had been divided due to the 1948 war and was re-united in the miraculous 6-day war of 1967, so the giant schism between mainline churches and Pentecostal denominations evaporated as the Holy Spirit was poured out during the Charismatic renewal movement of the same year[12].

1967 is also seen by many as the birth of the modern Messianic movement[13]. This movement is at the forefront of the restoration within both Israel and the Church. Firstly, it is bringing Jews both inside and outside Israel to faith in Jesus in the greatest numbers seen since the days of the Book of Acts. Secondly, the Messianic Movement is now beginning to impact Church teachings on a global scale, helping restore Christendom to its original Hebraic heritage.

The Jubilee is Not Complete

We are certainly living in an unprecedented age of restoration. Yet the Jubilee is by no means complete, far from it. Israel's land borders are still short of what God promised Abraham (Gen. 15:18–21), almost half of the world's Jews still live outside the Promised Land, and the spiritual state of the nation is far from the relationship with God promised in Scripture. The Church on the other hand is still waiting and praying for Jesus' Promised Return with all the glory it will bring.

Why then has this modern-day Restoration of Israel and the Church been taking place?

I believe one reason is that it is setting the stage for end time events. Jesus said He would not return until the Jews in Jerusalem welcome Him back with the Messianic cry "*Blessed is He who comes in the Name of the Lord"* (Luke 13:35). During the long centuries of Jewish exile, this prophecy simply could not be fulfilled. That is, until 1967. With the Jews back in Jerusalem, and with Messianic Jews telling their neighbours about the Messiah, the stage is now increasingly ready for the fulfilment of this prophecy.

Jesus also said He would not return until this gospel of the Kingdom is *"preached in all the world as a witness to all the nations"* (Matt. 24:14). For centuries the Church had no sense of urgency regarding preaching the gospel. For example, when William Carey spoke of going to India as a missionary in 1787, he was told *"Young man, sit down! When God pleases to convert the heathen, He will do without your aid or mine!"*[14] Thankfully today the Church has a much clearer sense of mission, and organisations such as Wycliffe are spearheading the way to translate the Bible into all languages of this world. As of writing, Bible translation is currently happening in 3,283 languages in 167 countries[15]. The Church is finally embracing its role to be a witness to this world, and this too is clearly bringing us ever closer to the Return of Jesus.

A Foretaste of the Jubilee

Another reason the Restoration of Israel and the Church has been taking place, is to give God's people a foretaste of the Jubilee. The miracles of Jesus' First Coming pointed to the coming Jubilee, whetting the people's appetite for what is to come. Likewise, the modern-day Restoration gives us hope that that God can and will restore His people, and that the ultimate Redemption is drawing nearer. Importantly, it shows us that God has not given up on His people Israel, nor has He given up on His Church. We both need restoration, and in His mercy, it has already begun.

The Restoration of Israel and the Church is a sign. For those of us who can read its message, it urges us to prepare ourselves, for the King is surely coming soon.

Insights from the Calendar

In our next chapter we will study the Calendar of Feasts God gave the Jews as we look for further clues about Jesus' second coming, the timing of the Jubilee and practical advice on how to prepare ourselves for what lies ahead.

¹ Dio Cassius, *History of Rome*, 69.14.1-2. Quoted in Wikipedia, *Bar Kokhba revolt* https://en.wikipedia.org/wiki/Bar_Kokhba_revolt (accessed Aug. 23, 2023)

² Kestenbaum, Sam. *When Martin Luther Accused The Jews Of Eating Satan's S—-,* https://forward.com/news/386479/when-martin-luther-accused-the-jews-of-eating-satans-s/(accessed Sep 24, 2024)

³ Quoted in *The First Zionist Congress*, Friends of Zion Museum, https://fozmuseum.com/blog/first-zionist-congress/ (accessed Aug. 22, 2023)

⁴ Curry, Jill. *Timing.* https://beersheba100.com.au/biblical-foundations/significance/the-timing.html (accessed Sep. 5, 2023)

⁵ *Balfour Declaration*, Wikipedia, https://en.wikipedia.org/wiki/Balfour_Declaration (Accessed Aug. 2, 2023)

⁶ Gold, Dore,*The Historical Significance of the Balfour Declaration ,* Jerusalem Center for Public Affairs. https://jcpa.org/article/historical-significance-balfour-declaration/ (accessed Aug. 2, 2023)

⁷ This is why the area today is called the 'West Bank', as it was the area controlled by Jordan west of the Jordan river.

⁸ Mitchell, Chris. *Israel's 1967 Miracle*, Jerusalem Dateline, CBN. Aired June 05, 2007

⁹ Sinensky, Tzi. *When Rav Goren Ascended the Temple Mount: For the 50th Yom Yerushalayim*, Sefaria. https://www.sefaria.org/sheets/67703.27 (accessed Aug. 22, 2023)

¹⁰ Oren, Michael. *Six Days of War: June 1967 and the Making of the Modern Middle East,* page 246. Quoted in Lavender, Enoch. *Rebuilding the Temple: Preparing for the Lord's Return,* 2022.

¹¹ *All embassies should be moved to Jerusalem* - editorial, Jerusalem Post, May 19, 2023. https://www.jpost.com/opinion/article-743506 (accessed Aug. 22, 2023)

¹² You can read more about this parallel restoration in Appendix C

¹³ The Messianic movement is a movement of Jews coming to faith in Jesus as the Messiah and studying the scriptures from a Jew-

ish understanding. This approach is bringing fresh understanding of the Scriptures to Jews and Gentiles alike.

[14] Brown, Dustin. *When God Chooses to Convert the Heathen, He Will!,* May 13, 2020, Vision Baptist Missions Inc. https://visionmissions.org/biographies/when-god-chooses-to-convert-the-heathen-he-will/ (accessed Sep. 5th, 2023)

[15] *2023 Global Scripture Access*, Wycliffe Global Alliance. https://www.wycliffe.net/resources/statistics/ (accessed Sep. 5th, 2023)

Reflection Questions

1. Has God rejected Israel? Explain why or why not using your own words.
2. Why do you think God has been restoring both Israel and the Church over these last 150 years?
3. What restoration remains to be fulfilled and how will it come about?

13

The Divine Calendar

Imagine for a moment that you were one of the many impoverished farmers in ancient Israel eagerly awaiting the coming of the Jubilee. Obviously you would be counting down the years, months and days to the time when you finally enter the 50th year. As the 49th year finally comes to a close, and New Year's eve arrives, you suddenly hear the unmistakable sound of a shofar blast resounding from Jerusalem' Temple. "This is it", you think to yourself. "I am free from my debts, and I am heading home!" However, you wouldn't get very far at all. Why? Because this trumpet blast is not the Jubilee trumpet, and the Jubilee is never announced on the Jewish equivalent of New Year's day. Confused?

In this chapter we are going to dive into an overview of the divine calendar, finding out on which feast day the Jubilee is announced and uncovering the prophetic significance of its unusual timing.

Introducing the Divine Calendar

Through Moses, God gave the Jews a divinely ordained calendar centred around seven annual feasts. The Lord describes them as "*My feasts*" (Lev 23:1) and as such they are significant for all believers to understand and study. The Hebrew word for "*feast*" can be better translated as a "*divine appointment*" or as "*prophetic dress rehearsals*"[1].

The first feast of the calendar is the Passover. On this day each year families would slay a lamb in remembrance of their forefather's miraculous deliverance from bondage in Egypt. This divine appointment was an annual prophetic picture pointing to Jesus, the ultimate Lamb of God. And it was no co-incidence that it was on this very day, as the Passover lambs were being sacrificed, that Jesus was crucified and died to set His people free from sin.

The next feast on the calendar is the Feast of Unleavened Bread (representing sinlessness) during which Jesus was in the tomb. Then followed the Feast of First Fruits, which marks the day Jesus rose again. This annual celebration involved farmers bringing their first fruits to God in faith that He would protect and bless the remainder of the Harvest as it grew and ripened. In this sense, the Resurrection of Jesus on First Fruits carries a significant promise that God will preserve all believers in Him for the Resurrection to come.

50 days after Passover, is the Biblical Feast of Pentecost. And it was on this foreordained day that the Holy Spirit was poured out on the disciples enabling them to boldly proclaim the message of the Messiah.

It is remarkable that God ordained these four feasts roughly 1500 years ahead of time to graphically and in order portray these key events of Jesus' First Coming. Today there remains three unfulfilled feasts, which listed sequentially are the Feast of Trumpets, the Day of Atonement and finally the great Feast of Tabernacles. These remaining feasts give us a unique grid to study Jesus' Return and the context of the coming fulfilment of the Jubilee.

A Preview of the End

The Feast of Tabernacles is the last feast on the calendar, and it has clear correlations to the Jubilee. Firstly, it is celebrated in the 7th month and lasts for 7 days, with one final day of celebration added at the end, reminiscent of the pattern of the Jubilee being celebrated the year after 7 x 7 years of agricultural cycles.

The Feast of Tabernacles is known in Judaism as "*The Time of our Rejoicing*", and it was stated that if you had never witnessed the joy of its exuberant celebration in the Temple, then it would be as if you had never experienced joy in your life[2]. This lively and euphoric celebration points us to the great joy of the final Jubilee. It points to the time when Israel will be back in her land, celebrating the agricultural blessings God has given her. It points to the glorious day when God Himself will 'tabernacle' among His people, and dwell amongst them once more (Rev. 21:3). In that day, there will be no more sorrow, and no more tears. Perhaps this is why at Tabernacles God's people were commanded no less than three times to rejoice before the Lord (Lev. 23:40, Deut. 16:14 and 15). In summary, Tabernacles is a prophetic celebration pointing to the great joy that lies ahead in Israel's future.

But how does Israel arrive at this moment of great joy which God has promised? Will this Jubilee just suddenly come all by itself, or is something required first for Israel?

We have seen in the previous chapter how God has already begun restoring Israel, but through the feasts we are going to discover that there is a pathway yet for Israel to travel before she can see the final fulfilment of God's promises. This pathway is revealed through the two feasts immediately preceding Tabernacles, namely the Feast of Trumpets and the Day of Atonement.

The Feast of Trumpets

The Feast of Trumpets is dedicated, as per its name, to the sounding of the ancient shofar. The Jewish civil year starts on this day[3], and if you had been among those waiting and longing for the 50th year Jubilee to arrive, no one would blame you for thinking the Jubilee would be announced on this day. However, this is not the case.

Instead, the Feast of Trumpets begins an intense time of repentance on the Jewish Calendar known as "*the Days of Awe*"[4]. The Feast of Trumpets is an annual wake up call urging God's people to repent in the lead up to the Day of Atonement. Occuring ten days later, this divine appointment is the most sacred day on the entire Jewish calendar.

And it is on this uniquely holy and solemn day that the Jubilee is proclaimed:

> Then you shall cause the trumpet of the Jubilee to sound on the **tenth day of the seventh month**; on the **Day of Atonement** you shall make the trumpet to sound throughout all your land.
> (Lev 25:9, emphasis added)

The Day of Atonement

As the holiest day on the Jewish Calendar, the Day of Atonement is biblically described as a day to "*afflict your souls*" (Lev. 23:27, 32). This was understood to mean that the day was to consist of fasting and solemn repentance before God. While there are several other fast days on the Jewish Calendar, only the Day of Atonement is mandated by Scripture. The Israelite who failed to fast and repent on this day was to be "*cut off from his people*" (Lev. 23:29) and those who choose to work on this day would suffer the death penalty (Lev. 23:30)[5]

The Day of Atonement is taken seriously to this day in Israel. On this day, all flights will cease operating and Israel's airspace will even close to flights passing through. Public transport ceases to operate and all local TV and radio broadcasts fall silent. Workspaces and factories shut their doors, and tens of thousands of Jews will stream to the Western Wall in Jerusalem for prayers of repentance.[6] Annually, over 60% of Israeli Jews participate in this day's solemn fasting and repentance[6].

I believe the Day of Atonement is a prophetic dress rehearsal of the future day when Israel as a nation will cry out to God in repentance. And it is only then that the Jubilee restoration of Israel can be released to its full extent. It is only from that place of repentance that all God's prophecies and promises can be fulfilled in Israel.

The Time of Jacob's Trouble

The nature of mankind is that we don't normally turn wholeheartedly to God until we are totally desperate. The Bible speaks of a desperate day to come when Israel will face what is known as the *'time of Jacob's trouble'* (Jer. 30:7). The book of Joel describes the frightful sight of an overwhelming enemy army entering the land in that day:

> Blow the trumpet in Zion,
> And sound an alarm in My holy mountain!
> Let all the inhabitants of the land tremble....
> A people come, great and strong,
> The like of whom has never been;
> Nor will there ever be any such after them....
> A fire devours before them,
> And behind them a flame burns;
> The land is like the Garden of Eden before them,
> And behind them a desolate wilderness;
> Surely nothing shall escape them....
> Before them the people writhe in pain;
> All faces are drained of color.
> (Joel 2:1-6)

Zechariah similarly describes this overwhelming End Time invasion as bringing devastation to Jerusalem:

> For I will gather **all the nations to battle against Jerusalem**; The city shall be taken, The houses rifled, And the women ravished. **Half of the city** shall go into captivity, But the remnant of the people shall not be cut off from the city.
> (Zec. 14:2, emphasis added)

Interestingly, world powers are today increasingly calling for Israel's capital Jerusalem to be divided, believing it to be the key to a broad peace with the Muslim nations. According to Zechariah we will one day see a military invasion of Israel attempting to enforce this proposed division of the city. However, this invasion will be far from peaceful, and will instead unleash violent destruction upon the inhabitants of Jerusalem. Again, Zechariah gives us more details:

> And it shall come to pass in all the land, Says the Lord, "That two-thirds in it shall be cut off and die, But one-third shall be left in it....
> (Zec 13:8)

Daniel the prophet describes this time in history as "*a time of trouble, such as never was since there was a nation*" (Dan. 12:1), and it will continue until "*the power of the holy people has been completely shattered*" (Dan. 12:7).

At that time of distress, Israel won't be able to rely on the might of her army to save her, nor will her allies in the Western World be of any assistance. Her only solution will be found in the Lord. And in that day, a desperate cry will arise from the nation, as foretold by the prophet Joel:

> Blow the trumpet in Zion, Consecrate a fast,
> Call a sacred assembly; Gather the people,
> Sanctify the congregation, Assemble the elders,
> Gather the children and nursing babes;
> Let the bridegroom go out from his chamber,
> And the bride from her dressing room.
> Let the priests, who minister to the Lord,
> Weep between the porch and the altar;
> Let them say, "Spare Your people, O Lord,
> And do not give Your heritage to reproach,
> That the nations should rule over them....
> (Joel 2:15-17)

Everyone in Israel, regardless of their age or personal situation, will in that day lay aside everything in order to fast and pray for the Lord's mercy. I believe this will be the prophetic fulfilment of the Day of Atonement. And as the nation of Israel repents and cries out for mercy, God Himself will hear their cry and come to their aid.

Joel continues:

> But I will remove far from you the northern army,
> And will drive him away into a barren and desolate land
> (Joel 2:20)

The prophet Zechariah further explains:

> ....when (the nations) lay siege against Judah and Jerusalem..... "In that day," says the Lord, "I will strike every horse with confusion, and its rider with madness;"....
> In that day **the Lord will defend the inhabitants of Jerusalem**; the one who is feeble among them in that day shall be like David, and the house of David shall be like God, like the Angel of the Lord before them. It shall be in that day that I will seek to destroy all the nations that come against Jerusalem.
> (Zec 12:2-9, emphasis added)

Not only will God defend and fight for His people on that day, but He will receive and embrace the repentant remnant of Israel:

> I will bring the *one*-third through the fire,
> Will refine them as silver is refined,
> And test them as gold is tested.
> They will call on My name,
> And I will answer them.
> I will say, 'This *is* My people';
> And each one will say, 'The Lord *is* my God.' "
> (Zec 13:9)

Then, on that great future Day of Atonement, and stemming from the place of national repentance, the Jubilee Trumpet will sound. As Jesus appears in His glory in the sky, Israel's mourning will soon turn to tremendous joy as the Messiah finally ushers in the restoration of all things.

The Context of the Jubilee Restoration

The Restoration of Israel, and ultimately of the entire world will not happen until Israel repents and turns to God. They are like the small hinge on which the entire door of God's blessing and prophetic plan will turn.

Paul the Apostle describes what he calls "*the great mystery*" of Israel as a nation rejecting their own Messiah. But, he says, it is through their fall "*that salvation has come to the Gentiles*" (Rom. 11:11). And if their fall "*is the reconciling of the world, what will their acceptance be but life from the dead?*" (Rom 11:15).

The immeasurable blessing of salvation came to the world through Israel rejecting Jesus. It had to be so, and it is only through His death that we today have salvation and forgiveness of sins. According to Paul there is an equally unfathomable blessing in store when Israel is finally restored to God as a nation, which he calls "*life from the dead*" (Rom 11:15). In other words, Paul is clear that Israel's repentance will lead to nothing less than the long awaited Resurrection of the Dead.

Peter must have had this in mind addressed a gathering of his fellow countrymen in the Temple courts:

> "*repent therefore.... so that times of refreshing may come from the presence of the Lord, and that He may send Jesus Christ... whom heaven must receive until the times of restoration of all things which God has spoken by the mouth of all His holy prophets since the world began*"
> (Acts 3:19-21, emphasis added).

According to Peter, Jesus *must* remain in Heaven for now. His Return and the Restoration spoken of "*by all the prophets*", is waiting for Israel's repentance.

With this in mind, it is imperative for believers to pray for Israel and the Jewish people. We need to pray for God to remove the scales over their eyes so that they can turn back to Him (Rom. 11:25). We also should pray for the Jews who have already come to faith in Jesus as their Messiah and for their witness to their fellow countrymen. Israel has truly suffered greatly through the centuries, but the full comfort and restoration God has promised them will only come through her turning back to God.

[1] Biltz, Mark, *How the Father Carefully Orchestrated the Events Leading Up to the Resurrection,* Charisma News, Apr 19, 2019. https://www.charismanews.com/world/75961-how-the-father-carefully-orchestrated-the-events-leading-up-to-the-resurrection (accessed July 31, 2023)

[2] Howard and Rosenthal, *The Feasts of the Lord,* p. 140. quoting Mishnah Sukkah 5:1

[3] The Jewish calendar has a civil year starting in the month of Tishri (the 7th month) and a religious year starting in the month of Nissan (the 1st month).

[4] Howard and Rosenthal, *The Feasts of the Lord,* p. 108.

[5] Ibid, p120

[6] Gross, Judah Ari, *Tens of thousands visit Western Wall for final 'selichot' services before Yom Kippur* , The Times of Israel, Oct 4, 2022. https://www.timesofisrael.com/tens-of-thousands-visit-western-wall-for-final-selichot-services-before-yom-kippur/ (accessed July 31, 2023)

[7] *60% of Jewish Israelis Plan to Fast on Yom Kippur,* The Israel Democracy Institute, Oct. 7, 2019. https://en.idi.org.il/articles/28747 (accessed July, 31, 2023)

Reflection Questions

1. Which four feasts on the Jewish calendar were fulfilled in Jesus' first coming?
2. How is the Feast of Tabernacles related to the Jubilee?
3. What does the Day of Atonement teach us about entering the blessing of the Jubilee?

14

The God Who Doesn't Give Up

Replacement Theology holds that God has given up on the Jewish nation due to their many sins. In Israel's place, God chose us, the *wonderful* Christians. One obivous problem with this teaching is that the Church has its own long list of sins and failures. In fact, as we study Church history, we may begin to wonder if God will reject the Church as well and find someone better?

By contrast the Jubilee teaches that our God goes to the greatest length possible to save and restore. Despite the depth of Israel's fall and her rejection of the Messiah, Paul declares "*I say then, has God cast away His people? Certainly not!.. For the gifts and the calling of God are irrevocable.*" (Rom. 11:1, 29).

Through the long dark ages of Jewish exile, God has miraculously preserved His people, enabling them against all odds to survive wave after wave of relentless and demonic persecution. Then God began to restore them to their land, miraculously defending them in battle, despite the fact that they *still* had not received their Messiah. To this day, He remains actively at work in Israel, and we know that one day His patient work will pay off, as His people finally turn back to Him.

The message that God has not given up on the Jewish people, is a message of hope to our world and to our families. God hasn't given up on the prodigals of this world, and neither should we.

My spiritual grandmother, Anne, had a husband called Colin who stubbornly rejected anything to do with faith in God. She persisted in praying for and loving Colin over many decades. When Colin was in his eighties, aged and sick, his defensive walls to the faith finally came down. And to the surprise of everyone, he humbly prayed, confessed his sins and received Jesus. Only a few days later Colin passed away.

Anne did not give up on her husband Colin, and neither did God. May I encourage you to learn from Anne's example and not give up praying for and lovingly ministering to the people in your life who are not walking with the Lord?

God's Restoration in My Life

I believe the promises of freedom and blessings of the Jubilee are available to us today on a personal level through Jesus our Redeemer. However, like Israel we can only enter these blessings through the journey of repentance.

As a young man I struggled with an addiction to pornography. Drowning in my own feelings of guilt and condemnation I felt like giving up on myself. I had tried my hardest to change, I had promised never to do it again, but I just kept on failing. I felt alone, isolated and rejected, and was sure that God was just as mad with me as I was.

After struggling on my own for many years, I finally made one of the hardest decisions of my life: to open up and share my struggles with mature Christians I could trust. Through prayer and counselling, God led me through a three-step process of repentance and restoration.

Firstly, I was re-assured that God still loves me despite my many failings. I was reminded that Jesus died for me, knowing full well the sins I would commit, and despite of all my sins, He still was willing to pay the price. I was brought back to the story of the Prodigal Son (Luke 15:11-32), knowing that God is like the Father whose heart is yearning and waiting for me to repent and return to Him.

The second step was to confess my sins. The Bible says:

> If we confess our sins, He is faithful and just to forgive us our sins and to cleanse us from all unrighteousness. (1 John 1:9)

I used to ask myself "*what is just about God forgiving me my sins?*" One day, I had a vivid experience that helped me understand God's justice. I had caught up with a friend for coffee, and when I went to pay, the shop attendant refused my payment. "*What is going on?*", I asked curiously. The shop keeper explained that a stranger had already paid for my coffee. As I later pondered what had happened, I realised it would have been unjust for the shop to accept my money as it was already paid.

In the same way, Jesus has already paid for my sins. I would never have been able to pay for it myself, but even if I tried, God would not accept the payment. Why? Because the payment has already been made. This is why John declares that He is "faithful and *just*" to forgive our sins.

Having confessed my sins, and having received forgiveness, God led me to the final step of restoration. The Bible describes the Holy Spirit as our "comforter" (John 14:26). This word doesn't just mean one who wipes away our tears, but it also means one who inspires courage to take action. A vital step of my restoration to God was the comfort and courage the Holy Spirit gave me to believe that through Him I could live without sin, and through Him this habit in my life could be broken.

Paul the Apostle, who so boldly served Jesus, once declared "*There is now no condemnation for those who are in Christ Jesus*" (Rom. 8:1). He who had been guilty of great crimes against the Church, could now hold his head high. His sins had been washed away, he had been given a fresh start, and he could now move forward with confidence. During my restoration, the Holy Spirit likewise helped me back on my feet, totally removing the weight of condemnation from off my shoulders, and giving me courage to live for Jesus again.

I am deeply grateful to God for taking me through this personal journey of restoration.

If you too are struggling with bondage to sin, I want to encourage you that our God of restoration has certainly not given up on you.

If you are ready to begin your journey of repentance and restoration today, please pray this prayer with me:

> Dear Heavenly Father,
>
> I thank you for the great love you have for me. Despite my sins and failures, you are still stretching out your arms of love to me, and I come to you right now through Jesus your Son.
>
> Father, I confess my sins of..... and repent before you for committing them, resolving not to commit them again.
>
> In accordance with Your Word, I ask you now to forgive me.
>
> I thank you that you have taken away my condemnation, and I choose to accept your forgiveness and I forgive myself for my own actions.
>
> Wherever these sinful habits have been re-enforced through patterns set in my family history, I confess these sinful patterns as well including ..... and put them under the blood of Jesus my Saviour and Redeemer.
>
> Holy Spirit, I thank you that you are the great encourager. Thank you that through your power, I can live a new life, free from the chains and powers of sin. Thank you that the old things in my life have passed away, and I am right now a new creation in You.
>
> In Jesus mighty name,
>
> Amen

For more on this topic, and a practical 'how-to' of resisting the temptations of sin, take advantage of our free 7-part teaching resource "Finding Freedom" available at www.olivetreeministries.org.au/freedom.

I also highly recommend the book "Self-Deliverance" by Messianic Bible Teacher Rabbi Schneider available via major retailers.

Reflection Questions

1. Has God given up on His people Israel? Why or why not?
2. Are there people in your life that you have given up hope for? How can you pray for them today?

15

Back to the Garden

> God saw everything that He had made, and indeed it was very good.
> (Gen. 1:31)

God's creation was perfect. Over the course of five days God created a beautiful planet, filled with amazing creatures, beautiful wildlife and trees, plants and flowers in abundance. Then on day six, all of creation must have stood in wonder as God stooped down to the dust of the earth to form His crowning masterpiece, a man in His very own image. With loving care, God had prepared a special place for mankind to live, a garden called Eden, which means "delight". This magnificent paradise contained everything Adam and Eve could ever need. It was the place of the Tree of Life, and from this garden flowed a river (Gen. 2:10).

God would regularly walk through this place of delight, enjoying sweet times of fellowship with the man He had created. Man and woman lived together unashamed of their nakedness, as there was no sin to cover up or hide. In this beautiful paradise, there was no suffering, no disease, no sorrow and no death.

God gave man specific tasks to do in the garden. Man was appointed to rule and have dominion over *"the fish of the sea, over the birds of the air, and over the cattle"* (Gen. 1:26). Specifically, He was to *"tend and keep"* the garden, the plot of land God had given him (Gen. 2:15).

Any gardener knows that for best results, a garden needs constant upkeep and vigilance, keeping weeds at bay. And this is where Adam failed. He should have been guarding the garden and not have permitted the serpent to enter, but instead the snake slipped right past him and begun its deceptive work on Eve. Soon both Adam and Eve had sinned, and immediately feelings of guilt and shame entered the world. Desperately trying to cover up their nakedness, Adam and Eve hid as they heard the familiar sound of God walking through the garden. Their fellowship was Him was broken, as revealed in God's haunting words "*Where are you?*" (Gen. 3:9).

Being separated from God, the source of life, death naturally entered the human race. And as a result of their sin, God was forced to banish Adam and Eve from the Tree of Life and send them into exile, far away from the garden which He had so lovingly prepared for them. And behind them, the blazing swords of the cherubim were blocking their return.

Yet in the midst of this moment of great despair, God gave mankind a glimmer of hope. He spoke of the 'Seed' of the woman who would one day crush the head of the serpent, destroying evil and reversing the curse (Gen. 3:15).

Paradise Lost?

Is the Garden of Eden a case of "paradise lost", a closed chapter that will never be re-opened? Or will God one day restore mankind from exile back to the very same garden, just like the pattern revealed in the Jubilee?

When Jesus returns, He will usher in a 1'000 year reign of great glory, resurrecting the righteous dead, restoring Israel and the nations, multiplying food and wine in abundance, and rewarding His faithful saints with positions of authority in His Kingdom.

But, even in this Messianic era the curse from Eden will still be in effect, and neither will we be back in Paradise.

For instance, the Bible tells us that there will still be sin and death happening here on Earth during this reign:

> ...the one who dies at a hundred will be thought a mere child; the one who fails to reach a hundred will be considered accursed.
> (Is. 65:20, NIV)

The rebellious nature of sin will be on full display again at the end of the Millennium. Satan, being released from prison for a time, will again stir up many nations to join arms together against God and His people, but the fire of God will come down from Heaven and swiftly destroy this final rebellion (Rev. 3:9). Then will follow the Second Resurrection, which is the time of judgment for the wicked[1].

A Garden or a City?

After the Millennium, we reach the final stage of God's master plan of restoration:

> Now I saw a new heaven and a new earth, for the first heaven and the first earth had passed away. Also there was no more sea. Then I, John, saw the holy city, New Jerusalem, coming down out of heaven from God, prepared as a bride adorned for her husband. And I heard a loud voice from heaven saying, "Behold, the tabernacle of God is with men, and He will dwell with them, and they shall be His people. God Himself will be with them and be their God. And God will wipe away every tear from their eyes; there shall be no more death, nor sorrow, nor crying. There shall be no more pain, for the former things have passed away."
> (Rev. 21:1-4)

There is some debate among scholars over whether these verses are referring to a "brand new" Heaven and Earth, or simply a radically renewed version. Either way, God's Holy City will come down from Heaven to Earth, bringing us into a paradise like state not seen since the Garden of Eden:

- God will finally dwell among us on Earth just like originally intended.
- As in the Garden of Eden, there will be no sickness, pain, sorrow or death.
- Our access to the Tree of Life and the River of Life will be restored (Rev. 22:1-2).

This ultimate restoration will be spectacular, but in our context of the Jubilee there remains one confusing question: Since we were exiled from a *garden*, why are we being brought to a *city* and specifically to New Jerusalem?

The Mystery of the City

To Westerners, Jerusalem is just another city. On an international scale, it is a small city, with no natural resources; hardly worth mentioning. Yet Jerusalem is truly a city like no other.

Both in Biblical Times as well as in modern Judaism, Jerusalem commands a central focus for the Jewish people. Every year at Passover and on the Day of Atonement they declare "*next year in Jerusalem, the rebuilt*". Three times a day and also at the saying of grace at mealtimes, Orthodox Jews will turn to face Jerusalem and pray for its rebuilding and God's presence to dwell in it again[2].

Biblically, Jerusalem is important because it is the place God has chosen as His dwelling place. As the Psalmist says:

For the Lord has chosen Zion; He has desired it for **His dwelling place**: "This is **My resting place forever**; Here I will dwell, for **I have desired it**.
(Ps. 132:13-14, emphasis added)

God has uniquely chosen and delighted in Jerusalem like He once did with Eden. Is there a link though Eden and this mountain of the Lord's choosing? Could they actually be one and the same?

The Gihon Spring

Jewish tradition holds that when Adam left the Garden, he sat down in the river flowing out of Eden, immersing himself fully in this source of living water[3]. It was an act of repentance, expressing a deep desire to return to his former state of innocence, to return to the River of Life and the Tree of Life found in the Garden. Indeed in Judaism, this river is seen to ultimately have had its source in Heaven itself[4].

We learn from the account of Genesis that one of the rivers flowing from the Garden of Eden was the River Gihon (Gen. 2:13). It so happens that Gihon is the name of the main spring and water source for Jerusalem.

In the Old Testament, God commanded Jews who were coming to the Temple to worship to practice ritual immersion. As they immersed themselves, they would have carried in mind Adam's concept of repentance and identified with the same desire to re-connect with the River of Life as they immersed in water from the Gihon.

In her research, Archaeologist Jennifer Guetta has found scholars who believe that the Garden of Eden was on a mountain, which again invites comparisons to the Temple Mount. She writes:

God's throne was on the top, and a garden stood halfway up the mountain protected by two winged creatures, where God met man. In the garden stood the tree of life and the tree of knowledge of good and evil, and from God's throne flowed a river of life[5].

Speaking of the Temple Mount in Jerusalem and hinting at its links back to Eden, Jennifer Guetta writes:

> From the belly of the mountain of God came the river of life, the Gihon spring, which bubbled up and flowed towards the East to the Siloam pool... Before ascending the mountain the people had to go through water purification (in its waters)[6].

The waters flowing out from beneath the Temple gathered in the Pool of Siloam which was over 68 meters (or 225 feet) wide[7], literally allowing tens of thousands of Jews to immerse at once. This was needed as millions would be in attendance at the Feasts in Jerusalem, and all were required to immerse prior to ascending God's holy hill.

As the Psalmist says:

> Who may ascend into the hill of the Lord?
> Or who may stand in His holy place?
> He who has clean hands and a pure heart...
>   (Ps. 24:3-4)

Just as Adam sought to come back to God's Holy Hill and the Garden of Eden through immersion in water, so Jews were practicing the same ritual each time they came to the Temple, many believing that the waters of the Gihon were somehow connected to the original

River of Life in the Garden. This same concept of immersing in water for repentance is also played out in the New Testament practice of baptism.

Eden and the Temple

Drawing parallels between the Temple, Jerusalem and the Garden of Eden, Jennifer Guetta continues:

> When Solomon built the Temple... it also represented a place between Heaven and Earth, where God met man like in Eden and talked with him. The Temple was decorated like a garden with palm trees, lilies, flowers, lions and pomegranates. It was the place where man came to meet God after being cleansed from his sin through sacrifices, and immersion in water. In the center stood the tree of life, which some believe [represented]... the menorah itself, others see the palm tree on the walls as the tree of life. The two pillars at the entrance were the guardians of the garden. The throne of God, the "residing" presence of God, was in the back, where the Ark of the Covenant resided[8].

Spiritually speaking, as Jews were coming to the Temple to worship, they were therefore re-connecting with the Garden of Eden, the place hosting God's presence.

In Judaism it is believed that all of creation emanated from a stone in Eden known as the foundation stone, which is today located within the Islamic Dome of the Rock on the Temple Mount. This foundation stone is believed to be where the Holy of Holies was located and where the Ark of the Covenant stood in the ancient Temple. The Talmud further teaches that it was from this very site God gathered the dust to make man[9].

Could all this mean that the Garden of Eden is somehow connected to Jerusalem? Author Chris Parshall draws out more fascinating links between Eden and Jerusalem:

> **In Eden**, God passed judgement on the "first Adam" because of sin. Later, God exercised judgment **in Jerusalem** by permitting His own Son, the "second Adam", [to face judgment and die]. **In Eden** God graciously covered the couple's shame with animal skins (Gen. 3:21), prefiguring the necessity of blood sacrifice (**in Jerusalem**) for the covering of sin.[10]
>
> (emphasis added)

Furthermore it was in Eden that God promised the future crushing of Satan's head, by the bruised heel of the Messiah. It was on the mountains of Jerusalem that Abraham was tested and was about to offer His only son Isaac, when God intervened providing a substitute ram. And it was here, at the hill of Golgotha, that the victory over the ancient serpent was accomplished for ever in the death of Jesus. So the story of salvation which began at Eden was completed in Jerusalem, the city which mystically links back to the Garden.

The Two Jerusalems

We have seen how the Garden of Eden and the earthly City of Jerusalem are closely intertwined. Both functioned as the dwelling place of God, both had a river of living water for cleansing, and both were the place of judgment of sin and the covering of sin through sacrifice.

Paul the Apostle refers to a heavenly and an earthly Jerusalem (Gal. 4:25-26), and as such the Jerusalem on Earth with its fallenness and limitations, points us to a bright and glorious heavenly Jerusalem[11].

> And he carried me away in the Spirit to a great and high mountain, and showed me the great city, the holy Jerusalem, descending out of heaven from God.
> (Rev. 21:10)
> And he showed me a pure river of water of life, clear as crystal, proceeding from the throne of God and of the Lamb. In the middle of its street, and on either side of the river, was the tree of life... The leaves of the tree were for the healing of the nations. And there shall be no more curse... And they shall reign forever and ever.
> (Reb. 22:1-5)

When the New Jerusalem descends from Heaven, we are back at the beginning, being restored to the mountain of God. Here God will dwell among His people again and mankind will bask in His radiant glory, enjoying access to the Tree of Life and drinking freely from the River of Life. Like in the Garden, there will be no more death, no more sorrow and no more pain. And like in the Garden, we will be reigning with Him. Then we will have returned to our ancient inheritance and our true eternal home, destined for us from the beginning of creation, the Garden of God.

The God of Restoration

God is truly a God of restoration. The paradise He created in Eden will be restored, and those of us who remain faithful to Him, will be privileged to be brought back to inherit that amazing place after the Millennium reign.

That will be the final fulfilment of the Jubilee, the final fulfilment of the restoration spoken by the prophets of old.

In truth, the message of the End Times can all be summed up in one glorious theme - *the restoration of all things.*

As the Book of Revelation draws to a close bringing to a completion the final glorious restoration, our Messiah Jesus declares:

> It is done!
>
> I am the Alpha and the Omega, the Beginning and the End.
>
> I will give of the fountain of the water of life freely to him who thirsts.
>
> (Rev. 21:6)

[1] See our appendix on the Two Resurrections for more details

[2] *Jerusalem in Judaism.* Wikipedia. Available at https://en.wikipedia.org/wiki/Jerusalem_in_Judaism. (accessed Sep. 15, 2023)

[3] Milgram, Goldie. *Mikveh, Water and Higher Consciousness.* Reclaiming Judaism. Available at http://www.reclaimingjudaism.org/teachings/mikveh-water-and-higher-consciousness (accessed Sep. 15, 2023)

[4] It is interesting to note that the Hebrew word for Heaven is "*shamayim*" literally meaning "*there is water*" or "*a place of water*".

[5] Guetta, Jennifer. *Mountain of God & River of Life.* Israel Today. Sep. 18, 2022. Available at https://www.israeltoday.co.il/read/mountain-of-god-river-of-life/ (accessed Sep. 15, 2023)

[6] Guetta, Jennifer. *Mountain of God & River of Life.*

[7] Lora Gilb & Steve Law, *Complete Excavation Of Biblical Pool Of Siloam Announced.* Patterns of Evidence, Jan. 13, 2023 . Available at https://www.patternsofevidence.com/2023/01/13/complete-excavation-of-biblical-pool-of-siloam-announced (accessed Sep. 15, 2023)

[8] Guetta, Jennifer. *Mountain of God & River of Life.*

[9] *Foundation Stone.* Wikipedia. Available at https://en.wikipedia.org/wiki/Foundation_Stone. (accessed Sep. 15, 2023)

[10] Parshall, Craig. *Finding Eden.* Israel My Glory. Available at https://israelmyglory.org/article/finding-eden/ (accessed Sep. 15, 2023)

[11] The name Jerusalem in Hebrew is in the rare plural dual form. Just like we in English speak of a pair of eyes or a pair of legs, so the name Jerusalem literally means a "pair of Jerusalems".

Reflection Questions

1. Name three ways Jerusalem and the Garden of Eden are connected
2. How did Solomon's Temple point back to the Garden?
3. How does repentance connect to baptism and the river of life?

Appendixes

16

Appendix A: Calculating the End

In 1988, Edgar Whisenant published the book "*88 Reasons Why the Rapture Will Occur in 1988*". He was so certain the Rapture would occur according to his predictions that he confidently asserted "*Only if the Bible is in error am I wrong*" and going further, "*If there were a king in this country and I could gamble with my life, I would stake my life on Rosh Hashana [The Feast of Trumpets] 88*"[1]. The impact of his message was felt far and wide as 4.5 million copies of his book were sold. TBN Christian broadcasters re-arranged their tv schedule for the days of his prediction (Sep. 13-15, 1988), airing programs on the Rapture with instructions to those left behind. When Edgar's predictions failed to come to pass, he revised his dates first by a few weeks, then to the following year and then on to the following years[2].

Can we Calculate the Final Jubilee?

In this book we have seen how Jesus' First Coming was perfectly timed to the calendar of feasts which God had given His people some 1500 years in advance. We have further seen the many links between the Jubilee and Jesus' Return, making a strong case that Jesus will indeed return on a Jubilee year and specifically on a Biblical Feast Day in that particular year. Like Edgar Whisenant, it might be tempting for us to use this information to try to calculate a date for Jesus Return.

However, we firstly need to note that there is a large degree of uncertainty today surrounding the exact dates of the Jubilee cycles. Firstly, there is a rabbinic debate over whether the Jubilee's 50th year is also simultaneously the first year of the coming Jubilee cycle or not. The difference means that there are either 49 or 50 full years between each Jubilee cycle, significantly affecting any calculations. The Jubilee has also not been kept in Israel since at least the time of the destruction of the Second Temple in 70 AD, further complicating attempts at setting firm dates[3].

Just Don't Do It

Jesus specifically told us "*of that day and hour no one knows not even the angels of heaven, but My Father only*" (Matt. 24:36). Perhaps this is why God has allowed such uncertainty about where we are in the Jubilee calendar?

The Sages of Judaism, while eagerly anticipating the Coming of the Messiah[4], do not look kindly on date setters:

> Blasted be the bones of those who calculate the end, for [their listeners] would say, 'Since the predetermined time has arrived, and yet [the Messiah] has not come, he will never come.'
> (Sanhedrin 97b)[5]

Judaism teaches that one should always live in readiness for the Messiah's coming. In fact, the famous sage Rambam listed this expectation as one of the 13 core tenants of the faith. According to Rambam, if you are not living in constant expectation of the Messiah, it is tantamount to denying the faith all together[6]. This is why the incorrect predictions of date setters are so dangerous, as it leads people astray from what is an absolute essential component of faith, the belief in and the living for the Coming of the Messiah. Given the number of Christian date setters, is it time for Churches to adopt this position as well?

A Different Way of Living

Expecting the Messiah's Return is meant to change the way we live our lives. A story from the Talmud illustrates this well:

> Rabbi Eliezer says: Repent one day before your death.
> Rabbi Eliezer's students asked him: But does a person know the day on which he will die?
> He said to them: All the more so.. one should repent today lest he die tomorrow.
> (Shabbat 153a)[7]

In light of the Messiah's soon coming, it is important for us to take repentance seriously. We shouldn't be allowing sin to build up under the carpet, but like Rabbi Eliezer, we should daily examine ourselves, seeking to remain in right relationship with God and with the people around us.

In this appendix we have seen reasons why we should avoid trying to calculate the final Jubilee and Jesus Second Coming. We should rather live our lives daily in eager anticipation for Jesus' Return, lifting our eyes with excitement towards the great and glorious redemption to come.

[1] *Edgar C. Whisenant*, Wikipedia, https://en.wikipedia.org/wiki/Edgar_C._Whisenant (accessed 5th Aug. 2023)

[2] Pamela Starr Dewey, *Edgar Whisenant's 88 Reasons*. Field Guide to the Wild World of Religion. http://www.isitso.org/guide/whise.html (accessed 5th Aug. 2023)

[3] See Footnote 2, Davidson, Baruch S., *When Is the Next Jubilee Year?* https://www.chabad.org/library/article_cdo/aid/513212/jewish/When-Is-the-Next-Jubilee-Year.htm, (accessed 5th Aug. 2023)

[4] While the Rabbis are expecting the Messiah's imminent arrival to be His first coming, we Christians believe that He has already been and is returning for the second time. As one Rabbi said, "*When the Messiah comes, I will ask Him: Sir, have you been here before?*"

[5] Quoted by Shurpin, Yehuda. *Can I Calculate the Date of Moshiach's Arrival?* Chabad.org, https://www.chabad.org/library/article_cdo/aid/2705100/jewish/Can-I-Calculate-the-Date-of-Moshiachs-Arrival.htm (accessed 5th August 2023)

[6] Blumenfield, Mordechai. *Maimonides #12 - The Messianic Era,* Aish.com. https://aish.com/48929482/ (accessed 5th Aug. 2023)

[7] *Shabbat 153a*, The William Davidson Talmud (Koren - Steinsaltz), Sefaria.com. https://www.sefaria.org/Shabbat.153a.3 (accessed 29th Aug. 2023)

17

Appendix B: The Second Resurrection

When Jesus returns to Earth at the sound of the trumpet, "*the dead in Christ will rise*" (1 Thes. 4:16). Only at the end of Jesus' 1'000 year reign will the remainder be raised:

> "And [the resurrected saints] lived and reigned with Christ for a thousand years. But the rest of the dead did not live again until the thousand years were finished.
> (Rev. 20:4-5)

This is known as the Resurrection of Condemnation (John 5:29) and is for the purpose of judging the wicked.

But why will the unrighteous be raised from the dead if they are going to be judged anyway? A rabbinic story explains the answer in parable form:

> A king... had a fine orchard, and in it there were fine first fruits of a fig tree, and he stationed two guards in the orchard, one lame, who was unable to walk, and one blind...
> Sometime later the owner of the orchard came [back] to the or-

chard. He said to the guards: The fine first fruits of a fig tree that were in the orchard, where are they? The lame person said: Do I have any legs with which I would be able to walk and take the figs? The blind person said: Do I have any eyes with which I would be able to see the way to the figs?

What did the owner of the orchard do? He placed the lame person upon the shoulders of the blind person just as they did when they stole the figs, and he judged them as one.

(Sanhedrin 91 a,b)

Just as the blind man and the lame person needed each other to commit the crime, so body and soul co-operate to commit sin in this life. According to the Rabbis, this is the reason God will one day re-unite body and soul and judge the two together for the crimes committed during this life.

The Bible clearly teaches that both the righteous and the wicked will rise from the dead. The future judgment in the flesh for those who disobey God, should instill us all with a healthy sense of the fear of God.

Paul the Apostle expresses how this healthy fear motivated his ministry:

> I also count all things loss for the excellence of the knowledge of Christ Jesus my Lord, for whom I have suffered the loss of all things, and count them as rubbish, that I may gain Christ .... if, by any means, I may attain to the [first] resurrection from the dead. (Phil. 3:8-11, authors comment added)

As one of our best examples of the Christian walk, Paul teaches us to pursue Jesus and the coming First Resurrection above all else, rather than (God-forbid) only rising at the Second Resurrection. Following the Messiah in this life may come at a tremendous cost, even to the point of laying down our very lives. But as this book has demonstrated, a truly glorious future awaits those who remain faithful.

May we all be counted worth to attain to that first resurrection and to rule and reign with Jesus in the age to come.

Amen!

18

Appendix C: The Parallel Restoration

In Chapter 12 we began to see how God had been restoring Israel and the Church. In this appendix I have included more about this dual restoration and the fascinating behind the scenes stories of what God has been doing in our day and age. We are certainly living in exciting times of restoration!

Restoring a Pure Language

As Jews began to trickle back to Palestine in the late 19th century, one man named Eliezer Ben Yehuda had a vision to restore the ancient language of Hebrew back to a modern language. The returning Jews were weak and divided, but a common language would be central in helping them to unite into a modern nation.

Undeterred by his diagnosis of deadly tuberculosis at age 18, Eliezer dedicated himself to bringing the ancient language back to life. From 1881 to 1921, Eliezer worked up to 18 hour days as he tirelessly researched ancient languages looking for fragments of ancient Jewish words. Combining this with his knowledge of Biblical Hebrew, Ben Yehudah began to piece together a modern and practical language, which he ultimately published in a mammoth 18 volume dictionary. By the end of his life, Eliezer's efforts had paid off and Hebrew had become so widely used that it was recognised as one of three languages in British Palestine[1].

The prophet Zephaniah spoke of the day when God "… will restore to the peoples a pure language" (Zeph 3:9). While this verse definitely predicts the restoration of "a" pure language, which language is he speaking of?

The previous verse contains the clue. Zephaniah 3:8 is the only verse in the entire Hebrew Bible to contain every single letter of the Hebrew alphabet – including the special form of five unique letters that appear differently when they appear at the end of a word. It seems that this verse is a giant hint that the language prophesied to be restored in the very next verse, is none other than the Hebrew language itself.

The language of Hebrew was not the only language that was lost during the time of Israel's exile. In the early centuries of the church, the gifts of the spirit all but died out. However, in the late 18th century, many believers began to earnestly seek and pray for a new Pentecost, believing from their reading of the Scriptures that we were nearing the End of the Age. In response to these prayers, on New Years Eve 1901, there was an outpouring of the Holy Spirit in Topeka, Kansas evidenced by the speaking in tongues. This became the catalyst for of a mighty Pentecostal revival which swept the globe.

It is no accident that the restoration of the language of the Spirit to the Church happened precisely in the middle of the 40 year period in which Hebrew was being restored to the Jewish nation.

The God of the Bible is Not Dead

A tale is told of a Rabbi's son who witnessed a truck ferrying horrified Jews to the gas chambers of Auschwitz. In desperation, he cried out: *"God, stop this truck!"* But the truck did not stop, and the young man turned his back on the scene emotionally declaring "*There is no God.*" As a result of the Holocaust, a large number of Jews similarly questioned their faith. Where was the God of the Bible who had in ancient times displayed such power to save His people?

Only three years after the Holocaust, the infant state of Israel faced a perilous invasion from five modern Arab armies. Israel at the time had only 35,000 fighting men in its army. Its air force consisted of a single training aircraft from which a grenade could be thrown, and its army possessed only 6 tanks. The Egyptian army alone outnumbered the Israeli soldiers, with its over 60 planes and 135 tanks[2]. The distinguished U.S. Secretary of State and renown military genius, George Marshall, warned the Israelis that they would face annihilation and stood little to no chance. Furthermore, he made it clear that the US would not help the Israelis in such a war if they proclaimed statehood[3]. Despite these warnings, Israel's leader David Ben Gurion, forged ahead with declaring independence.

In the bitter war that ensued, 100,000 Jews in Jerusalem were placed under siege and cut off from outside food supplies for three months. Facing the real threat of starvation, the mayor of Jerusalem, Dov Yosef, imposed food rationing at the levels of Japanese concentration camps. At one point during the siege, an unseasonal rain fall caused the highly nutritious weed khubeiza to sprout up across the city. As they saw the weed, the local Jews proclaimed, "*God is with us, like in the days of Egypt*". The siege ended right as Jerusalem's supplies were down to their last day's ration of bread and only twelve hours of electricity[4].

As the ill equipped and heavily outnumbered Jewish defenders fought bravely and desperately, there were many tales of miracles on the battle field. One example is from the city of Safed in the north of the country, where the Arabs were encamped in a virtually impenetrable position. The Israelis had a very inaccurate, but extremely noisy mortar called the Davidka which they fired several times one Friday afternoon towards the Arab position. Shortly afterward there was an uncharacteristic rainfall in the area. Confused by the loud noise from the Davidka and the ensuing rain, the Arabs were convinced that the Israelis had an atom bomb and promptly fled their positions![5]

The God of Israel was truly back as the Jewish people experienced miracle after miracle of divine protection on the battlefield. 1948 thus marks the beginning of a new move of miracles in the Nation of Israel and a renewed faith in the God of miracles. In the words of Israel's founding Prime Minister David Ben Gurion, *"In Israel, in order to be a realist you must believe in miracles"*[6]

The Church had also lost faith in the God of miracles. For centuries it had been taught that healing was not for today and that it died out with the early apostles. However, in 1947, a ten-year revival known as the Voice of Healing Revival, broke out in the US which at its peak saw over 100 travelling evangelists pack thousands at a time into tent meetings across the nation[7]. Healings and miracles were suddenly brought back to central focus in the Church, at the very same time as Israel was experiencing miracles once again.

Walls of Division Come Crashing Down

In Israel's founding war of 1948, the Jews lost control of the Old City of Jerusalem while maintaining sovereignty over the newer parts of town. As a result, an internal border was erected through the battle-scared city, separating the Israeli side from the Jordanian controlled East Jerusalem.

In the miraculous 6-day war of 1967, West and East Jerusalem were re-united under Jewish rule, and at the same time significant developments of restoration began within the Church. 1967 marks the beginning of the Charismatic renewal, a move of Holy Spirit baptism, signs and miracles spreading to tens of millions throughout the mainstream churches. No longer were the gifts of the Holy Spirit the exclusive realm of the Pentecostals, and as a result the walls of division between the Pentecostals and other denominations began to come down. And all this was happening in the very same year that

Jerusalem's ugly internal border was being torn down, re-uniting the Holy City.

Living in the Days of Restoration

While the Bible certainly calls the time leading up to the return of Jesus "the End Times", it also calls it "the Time of the Restoration of All Things". And with our own eyes we are privileged to witness God's hand of restoration at work today in both the Church and in Israel. This should only continue to build our expectation as we eagerly anticipate the great and final Jubilee, the Day of the Final Redemption when all will finally be restored according to God's blueprint and design.

What a day it will be!

[1] See St. John, Robert, *Tongues of the Prophets: The Life Story of Eliezer Ben Yehudah,* Doubleday & Company Inc. Garden City, New York: 1952

[2] *Miracles – During the War of Independence,* Jewish History.org, https://www.jewishhistory.org/miracles-during-the-war-of-independence (accessed Aug 2, 2023)

[3] Collins L and Lapierre D., *O Jerusalem,* p. 316. New York, NY: Simon & Schuster Paperbacks, 1972

[4] Collins L and Lapierre D., p. 243.

[5] *Miracles – During the War of Independence*

[6] As quoted in *Israel : Years of Crisis Years of Hope* (1973) by Roman Frister, p. 45

[7] *The Voice Of Healing Revival 1948 - 1957,* Ancient Wells, https://jcpa.org/article/historical-significance-balfour-declaration/ (accessed Aug. 2, 2023)

Index of Topics

Afterlife – 38, 46, 55
Antiochus Epiphanes IV – see persecution
Antisemitism – 73-75, 97-98
Agricultural blessings – 19-20

Balfour Declaration – 99, 102
Baptism – 132-133

Eden (Garden of) – 127, 131-135

Feasts (of Israel) – 109
- Day of Atonement – 112, 116
- Feast of Tabernacles – 110-111
- Feast of Trumpets - 111
- Passover - 110
- Pentecost – 110

Hades – 55
Healing - 20

Gospel (of the Kingdom) – 13
Gnostics, Gnosticism – 38-41, 68

Heaven - 39-41, 45-46, 57, 65, 91-92, 130
Hebrew (restoration of) – 103, 149

INDEX OF TOPICS

HaTikvah (National Anthem of Israel) - 73
Holocaust – 67, 75

Israel's wars
- 1948 (Independence war) – 151
- 6-day war – 100, 103

Jericho (walls of) – 80
Jerusalem
- Destruction of – 74
- US Embassy – 101
- East Jerusalem – 100
- End time war - 113
- Food miracle - 151
- Future Kingdom of Jesus – 66, 73, 89
- Mount of Olives – 37
- Meaning of – 137 Footnote 11
- New Jerusalem – 130, 135
- Return of Jews to – 18, 79, 104
- Return of Jesus – 89, 103

Martin Luther – 98, 102
Miscarriage - 56
Mount Sinai – 33-35, 93-94

New Heaven and New Earth - 129

Pentecostal revival - 150
Persecution
- of Bible saints – 49
- of Christians – 27, 50
- of Jews (see Antisemitism)
Pornography (addiction) - 122

Rapture – 89, 93, 95 Footnote 3, 141
Reigning with Christ – 66-67
Regathering
- Of Israel – 75-80, 82-83, 87-89
- Of the Church - 90
- Trumpet Announcement - 80
Replacement Theology – 98
Resurrection – 21-22, 37-38, 46, 50, 55, 145
Resurrection body – 48

Shalom (definition of) - 69
Sheol – 55

Time of Jacob's Trouble - 113
Temple Mount – 100-101, 132-133
The Sound of Freedom (movie title) – 61
Theodor Herzl – 99

Vengeance (day of) – 8, 62

Wedding (of the Lamb) – 92
Wycliffe (Bible Translators) - 104

Yobel (Hebrew word for Jubilee) – 34, 80

Selected Bibliography

Collins L and Lapierre D. *O Jerusalem.* New York, NY: Simon & Schuster Paperbacks, 1972

Cumming, Greg. *The Milk Course.* Course available at www.milkcourse.org. I would also highly recommend his online interactive classes, available at www.thetorahportion.org

Howard and Rosenthal, *The Feasts of the Lord: God's Prophetic Calendar From Calvary to the Kingdom.* Nashville, TN: Thomas Nelson Inc, 1997

Lancaster, D. Thomas, *Elementary Principles: Six Foundational Principles of Ancient Jewish Christianity.* Marshfield, Missouri: First Fruits of Zion, 2014

Richardson, Joel. *When a Jew Rules the World: What the Bible Really Says about Israel in the Plan of God.* Leawood, Kansas: Winepress Media, 2015

Richardson, Joel. *Sinai to Zion: The Untold Story of the Triumphant Return of Jesus.* Leawood, Kansas: Winepress Media, 2020

Scheller, Gustav. *Operation Exodus: Prophecy being Fulfilled.* Bournemouth, England: Ebenezer Emergency Fund International, 1998

St. John, Robert, *Tongues of the Prophets: The Life Story of Eliezer Ben Yehudah,* Garden City, New York: Doubleday & Company Inc., 1952

Wright, Tom. *Surprised by Hope: Rethinking heaven, the resurrection and the mission of the Church.* London, UK: Society for Promoting Christian Knowledge, 2011

Other Books by the Author

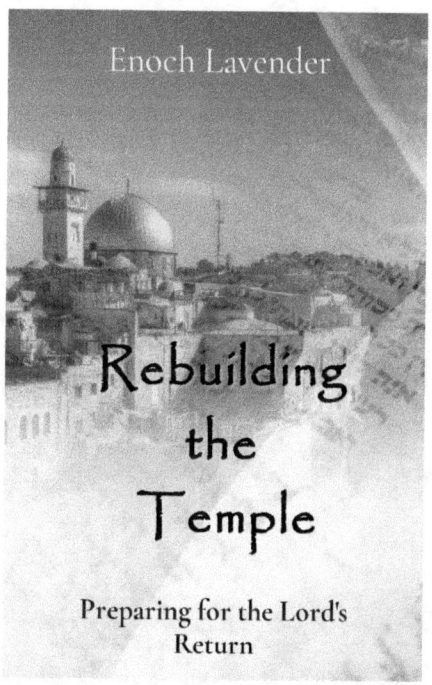

Rebuilding the Temple: Preparing for the Lord's Return chronicles recent developments regarding the Third Temple in light of its key role in Bible Prophecy. In this book, Ps. Enoch Lavender examines the challenging topic of the Abomination of Desolation as well as the surprising potential role of Islam in the rebuilding of the Temple. *Rebuilding the Temple* examines the miracles of the 6 Day War, the recent and unexpected rise of a Temple Mount advocate to Israel's national stage, and the reasons why the Temple – despite many obstacles – will one day be built.

Book available for order via Amazon, major Christian retailers as well as via www.olivetreeministries.tv

OTHER BOOKS BY THE AUTHOR | 163

Are you waiting for the fulfilment of a promise from God?

Have you at times lost hope and doubted that it will ever come to pass?

You are not alone!

In *Hope Fulfilled*, Enoch and Sarah Lavender share the highs and lows of their long journey towards marriage. They both had a sovereign promise from God, yet faced discouragement and disillusionment as they waited for its fulfilment. In this book, Enoch and Sarah share the life-changing lessons they learned along the way, as well as their encouraging testimony of God's faithfulness in fulfilling His promises.

Book available for order via Amazon, major Christian retailers as well as via www.olivetreeministries.tv

About the Author

Enoch and Sarah Lavender head up Olive Tree Ministries, an end time teaching ministry focused on the Jewish background of our faith.

Enoch has a B.A. in intercultural ministry from Harvest Bible College and has been studying Hebrew and the Jewish roots of our faith for over a decade.

Enoch and Sarah enjoy ministering to couples and young people, sharing their testimonies of love, forgiveness and God's redemptive plans. Enoch and Sarah live on the Gold Coast of Australia with their three young kids.

For a range of free teaching articles and videos, a free teaching newsletter and web store, see www.olivetreeministries.tv

Can you Help us?

Did you enjoy this book? Please consider leaving a review online with the book retailer from which you bought the book.

Your review will be of great help as we spread the message contained in *The Jubilee: Discover the End Time Mystery.*

www.ingramcontent.com/pod-product-compliance
Lightning Source LLC
Chambersburg PA
CBHW051435290426
44109CB00016B/1561